890L

ELDEN D. FINLEY
JR. HIGH SCHOOL LIBRARY

S0-ARM-161

DATE DUE

NOV 2 6 2012

ELLEN D. FINLEY
JR. HIGH SCHOOL LIBRARY

PRENTICE HALL
LITERATURE LIBRARY

Journey Home

Yoshiko Uchida

· · · ·

With
Connected Readings

PRENTICE HALL
Upper Saddle River, New Jersey
Needham, Massachusetts

Copyright © 2000 by Prentice-Hall, Inc., Upper Saddle River, New Jersey 07458. All rights reserved. No part of this book may be reproduced or transmitted in any form or by any means, electronic or mechanical, including photocopying, recording, or by any information storage and retrieval system, without permission in writing from the publisher. Printed in the United States of America.

ISBN 0-13-437493-2

1 2 3 4 5 6 7 8 9 10   03 02 01 00 99

PRENTICE HALL

Acknowledgments

Grateful acknowledgment is made to the following for permission to reprint copyrighted material:

Clarion Books/Houghton Mifflin Company
"Judith Steel" from *Hiding to Survive: Stories of Jewish Children Rescued from the Holocaust.* Copyright © 1994 by Maxine B. Rosenberg. Reprinted by permission of Clarion Books/Houghton Mifflin Company. All rights reserved.

Delacorte Press, a division of Random House, Inc.
"A Daughter of the Sea" by Maureen Crane Wartski, copyright © 1993 by Maureen Crane Wartski, from *Join in, Multiethnic Short Stories* by Donald R. Gallo, editor. Used by permission of Delacorte Press, a division of Random House, Inc.

Holiday House, Inc.
From *The Children of Topaz* by Michael O. Tunnell and George W. Chilcoat. Copyright © 1996 by Michael O. Tunnell and George W. Chilcoat. All rights reserved. Reprinted by permission of Holiday House, Inc.

Houghton Mifflin Company
From *Farewell to Manzanar* by James D. and Jeanne Wakatsuki Houston. Copyright © 1973 by James D. Houston. Reprinted by permission of Houghton Mifflin Company. All rights reserved.

Kelsey Street Press
"Can't Tell" from *Dreams in Harrison Railroad Park* by Nellie Wong, published by Kelsey Street Press. Reprinted by permission of Kelsey Street Press.

Lee & Low Books, Inc.
"Baseball Saved Us" by Ken Mochizuki. Text copyright © 1993 by Ken Mochizuki. Reprinted by permission of Lee & Low Books, Inc., New York, NY 10016.

(Acknowledgments continue on p. 122.)

Contents

Journey Home

Yoshiko Uchida

Connected Readings

Journey Home

Journey Home

Yoshiko Uchida

Chapter 1

I CAN'T see, Yuki thought frantically. I can't breathe.

The screaming desert wind flung its white powdery sand in her face, stifling her and wrapping her up in a smothering cocoon of sand so fine it was like dust. It blinded her and choked her and made her gag as she opened her mouth to cry out.

The black tar-papered barracks on either side of the road had vanished behind the swirling dust, and Yuki was all alone in an eerie, unreal world where nothing existed except the shrieking wind and the great choking clouds of dust. Yuki stumbled on, doubled over, pushing hard against the wind, gasping as she felt the sting of sand and pebbles against her legs.

Suppose she never got back to her barrack? Suppose the wind simply picked her up and flung her out beyond the barbed wire fence into the desert? Suppose no one ever found her dried, wind-blown body out there in the sagebrush?

A cry of terror swelled up inside her. "Mama! Papa! Help me!"

The sound of her own scream woke her up. Yuki's heart was pounding. Her damp fists were clenched tight. Her face was wet with tears.

For several minutes she couldn't believe it was only a nightmare. It had all seemed so real, she could almost taste the flat, powdery dust in her mouth. She had been back in the Utah desert, living with Mama and Papa and her big brother, Ken, in Topaz, one of the World War II concentration camps where all the Japanese of the West Coast had been sent by the government.

Yuki shuddered and blinked hard, trying to see where she really was. Was she back in the small crowded barrack room where their four army cots were separated by army blankets strung on ropes? Would she have to wake Mama and ask her to bring the flashlight and go out to the latrine with her because she was too scared to go alone? Would she have to rush from toilet to toilet to find one that wasn't filled with filth because the water had stopped running?

Yuki gathered herself up into a small ball and hugged her knees. Gradually, slowly, she left the strange world of dreams and nightmares and knew she was safe in her room in the apartment in Salt Lake City, which the minister of the Japanese church had found for them. And he'd told them not to worry because the landlady, Mrs. Henley, didn't mind their being Japanese.

For a few moments Yuki remembered again the awful fear that had consumed her those last weeks in Topaz when Papa had been threatened by the small gang of agitators. They had turned their anger at being in camp against anyone who, like Papa, worked with the administration to keep the camp running smoothly. And finally, one night, they had thrown a stink bomb into their barrack room. After that both Mama and Papa knew it was no longer safe to remain in camp, even though they wanted to stay and do whatever they could to help their people.

"Your family has already spent almost a year in camp," the director had said to Papa. "I think it's time now that you left."

He had secured special clearance for them to leave, and they had gone to Salt Lake City as soon as possible. Now they were safe outside the camp, and there was no more barbed wire fence to keep them from going anywhere they wanted to go.

Yuki took a deep breath and wiped her nose with the corner of the sheet. Mama wouldn't like her doing that, but she was still too shaky to get out of bed. She stared into the darkness until she could make out the familiar things in her room: the big, carved-oak chest of drawers that Mrs. Henley's great-grandfather had built, the small, chintz-covered armchair that was Yuki's favorite chair in the whole apartment, and the large gold frame on the wall with the watercolor scene of sailboats in a sunny harbor.

Yes, everything was all there. It was all right. She was safe, and she needn't ever worry again about being blown into the desert to turn into a heap of sun-bleached bones.

But her best friend, Emi Kurihara, wasn't safe, Yuki reminded herself. Emi and her grandma had been their neighbors in camp, and they were still out there in that awful desert with its duststorms and scorpions and the guard towers and the fence.

"You'd just better hurry up and come on out," Yuki said now to Emi.

Yuki often carried on conversations with people who were hundreds of miles away, because she felt if she just concentrated hard enough the message from her brain would somehow reach theirs, no matter where they were. It was most convenient, because she could talk to Emi in Topaz, or to her brother fighting in Italy with the 442nd Regimental Combat Team, or even to her old friend Mrs. Jamieson back home in Berkeley, California. And she always had the feeling that somehow each of them got her messages.

"Don't worry," she continued to Emi. "Papa will help you and your grandma get out of camp. He said he would."

If he promised, Yuki knew he'd try. With that reassuring thought, she suddenly sat up in bed. She was famished, and she began to think about juicy hamburgers and french fries and chocolate milk shakes.

Her stomach gurgled noisily as she pulled on her bathrobe and slid into her slippers. She walked carefully toward the kitchen, giant-stepping over the boards that squeaked so she wouldn't awaken Mrs. Henley or her invalid husband or their two Siamese cats downstairs. Mrs. Henley had already warned Yuki that she was a light sleeper and could hear every night sound in the entire house.

The kitchen still smelled faintly of chicken and soy sauce, and Yuki wished she hadn't eaten the last piece at supper so there would have been some left for her now. She stared into the cold whiteness of the refrigerator and contemplated the brown paper bag with her lunch for tomorrow.

"Should I?" she asked herself.

"I should," she answered. What was wrong with putting half the baloney sandwich in her stomach right now when she was starving, instead of leaving it for tomorrow.

She sat down at the table and quickly undid the wax paper wrapping, surprised at all the noise it made in the silent kitchen.

She had just taken a bite when she heard the creak of the floor in the hallway. Yuki groaned softly. Now Mrs. Henley would probably pop out of bed and stay up the rest of the night with her cats. Then tomorrow she'd tell Yuki she'd lost an entire night's sleep because of the night sounds.

Yuki turned and saw that it was Papa. The hair over his bald spot was rumpled, and he squinted sleepily without his glasses.

"Well, Yuki," he said with a slow smile. "Since when do you eat your lunch at three o'clock in the morning?"

Yuki swallowed and grinned sheepishly. "I had the most hor-rible nightmare," she explained.

"Were you back in Topaz?"

Yuki nodded. "In the most awful dust storm! I was lost, and I couldn't breathe, and I thought I'd never see you or Mama again."

She shuddered as the despair of her nightmare overwhelmed her once more.

Papa sat down at the table beside her and patted her hand. "It's strange," he said slowly. "I just had a vivid dream too."

"About Topaz?"

Papa poured himself some milk and buttered a piece of bread. "No, mine was a pleasant dream. We were home in Berkeley and we were in the backyard by the peach tree, you and I, trying to give Pepper a bath with the hose. Remember how he'd shake himself and spray everything within fifty feet with all that soap and water?"

Papa smiled as though he were seeing it all happening in front of him now.

Yuki grinned too, remembering. "And I'd get soap and water in my eyes and mouth and get soaking wet and . . ."

Suddenly a sharp deep longing to go back home to Berkeley flooded over her. "Papa, when can we go back?"

"I hope when the war is over, Yuki. When the United States and Japan stop fighting each other. When the hate is gone. Then maybe . . ."

"Only maybe?"

Papa rubbed his eyes and sighed. "Well, the Japanese are still excluded from the West Coast by law, and there are some people in California who don't want us ever to go back. They would have us kept out of the state forever."

"Forever?"

Was Papa saying they might never get to go home again? What would happen then to the thousands of Japanese who'd been uprooted from their homes and businesses and farms along the West Coast and were still in the concentration camps? Where would they all go if they couldn't go home to California after the war?

And what about us, Yuki wondered. Suppose they could never go back home. She couldn't bear even to think of such a thing. She thrust out her chin and said defiantly, "Well, I'm going back to California because that's where I was born, and that's where I belong, and nobody's going to keep me out!"

Papa gave her a look that held both surprise and pleasure.

"Good for you, Yuki," he said. "You hold onto that good thought, and maybe one day it will all come about."

Chapter 2

YUKI hated coming home from school on Tuesdays. That was one of the days Mama went to help Mrs. Griswold clean her house, and she wouldn't be home when Yuki got there. The apartment would be silent and empty, and Yuki would have to let herself in and sit in the lonely emptiness until Mama got home.

At least let there be some good mail today, she thought, and all the way home she sent messages to the mailbox to be stuffed with nice fat letters for her.

When she got home, she found their landlady, Mrs. Henley, sitting on the front porch with her husband. They were sitting in their rockers, each holding a Siamese cat, and watching the world go by.

"Afternoon, Yuki," Mrs. Henley called out.

"Hi, Mrs. Henley, Mr. Henley."

The old man was bundled up in a plaid blanket, looking like a race horse who'd just won a race. Mrs. Henley was keeping the autumn chill off his bones, she explained.

Yuki knew Mrs. Henley wanted to chat, but she could already see something in the mailbox and she longed to find out what it was. Besides, she wasn't crazy about chatting with Mrs. Henley, even though she did look the tiniest bit like her old friend, Mrs. Jamieson, who lived across the street from them in Berkeley. It was probably her pale crepey skin and the gray-green eyes. But of course her eyes didn't have the friendly warmth of Mrs. Jamieson's, and she didn't have the bright halo of flaming hair that Mrs. Jamieson dyed each month in remembrance of her late husband, Captain Jamieson, who had told her never ever to change. Mrs. Henley couldn't come close to being like Mrs. Jamieson, not in a million years.

Yuki thought longingly of the cozy warmth of Mrs. Jamieson's house with its scent of rose petals and spices, and of the hot cocoa they'd sip together as they looked at her collections of stamps and seashells and jewels. The day before Yuki and her family got sent to camp, Mrs. Jamieson had taken a beautiful gold and pearl ring from her jewelry box and given it to Yuki.

"Keep this for good luck, Yuki, dear," she'd told her, "and I know one day you'll come back home again."

But Yuki was afraid to take the ring into camp with her for fear she might lose it. Mama was storing all her valuables in a trunk at Bekins Van and Storage, so Yuki put her ring in its black velvet box, then inside a pair of socks, and put it in Mama's trunk too.

There were a lot of things besides her valuables in Mama's trunk. There were things like packets of faded letters from her family in Japan, old diaries and photograph albums, and the drawings and clay animals that Ken and Yuki had made in grammar school. Mama saved everything. She couldn't bear to throw out anything that was special to her. So when the President of the United States ordered all the Japanese out of the West Coast, and the army gave them ten days to leave Berkeley, Mama didn't know where or how to begin.

"How can I pack our whole life into boxes and cartons in just ten days?" she asked desperately. "If only Papa were here."

But Papa was in a prisoner of war camp in Montana where he and hundreds of other Japanese businessmen and community leaders had been sent by the FBI the day the war broke out. All he could do was write letters that arrived full of holes cut out by the censors.

Mama grew more and more frantic as she counted the days until they had to leave. She put a "Furniture for Sale" sign in the front window and sold her nice sofa and dining room set to the first woman who inquired. She sold and gave away things she should have stored and stored things she should have thrown out.

She was so careful to obey every new order issued by the government that she even insisted Ken take his binoculars and camera to the police station when the Japanese were told to turn in all "contraband."

Ken was among the first to go and register as "head of household," and when he came home he had a handful of numbered baggage tags that were to be attached to everything they were permitted to take into camp.

"Look," he said dismally. "We're Family 13453 now."

Yuki tried out the sound of it and hated it. "Yuki Sakane, Number 13453." It made her feel like a prisoner.

Some nights, Yuki's best friend in Berkeley, Mimi Nelson, came from next door to see her, since Yuki could no longer go out after the eight o'clock curfew set for all Japanese.

"It's so stupid!" Mimi said indignantly. "What do they think you'd do after eight o'clock anyway?"

"Maybe go out and shoot somebody," Yuki answered dourly.

But Ken added quickly, "It's a lot more likely somebody'd take a shot at us!"

He was right. There were plenty of people in California who

hated anybody with a Japanese face, and many of them carried guns. In fact, the parents of one of his college classmates had been shot and killed by vigilantes in one of the small valley towns.

On their last day in Berkeley, it was Mimi Nelson's mother who drove them to the civil control station where the Japanese of Berkeley were to report to be taken to camp. As they were leaving, Mrs. Jamieson hurried from across the street to say goodbye. She pinned a pink carnation from her garden on Mama's coat, saying, "I hope you'll be coming home soon, my dear."

Then she turned to Yuki and gave her a long, wordless hug. The last thing Yuki said to her was, "I stored your ring in Mama's trunk, Mrs. Jamieson. I'm saving it to wear when we all come home again."

And somehow that promise and the thought of the tiny gold ring waiting in its velvet box in the darkness of the trunk gave Yuki the hope that they really would go home again one day.

Yuki could never begin to love Mrs. Henley the way she loved Mrs. Jamieson, even though on the day they moved in, she had brought them a hot tuna noodle casserole.

She had the feeling that Mrs. Henley never quite trusted them. Once she'd asked Yuki why they had been sent to the concentration camp in the first place.

"Why would the President make all the Japanese leave the West Coast if you weren't dangerous?" she asked.

"Papa says there were a lot of reasons," Yuki explained. "It was partly panic and partly because there've always been people in California who wanted to get rid of us."

Mrs. Henley pursed her lips. "Well, it's possible you people might have tried to help Japan. After all, it *is* your country."

"But it's *not* my country. The United States is," Yuki said impatiently.

"But why would your own country put you behind barbed wire?"

"They never should have."

"Weren't there some Japanese who sent signals from their fishing boats?"

"No! Those were lies."

How could Mrs. Henley believe those stupid rumors? Yuki wished Ken were there to help explain everything to her. He'd know how. She tried hard to think what Ken might say.

"My brother Ken volunteered for the army from camp," she said, her voice rising, "even if his country put him in a concentration camp."

Mrs. Henley's eyebrows arched up in surprise. "He did?"

"Sure. So did his friend, Jim Hirai. They both went."

Yuki had never felt good about Mrs. Henley after that conversation. It had left her feeling bruised and let down. Mrs. Henley had not only disappointed her, she'd left Yuki feeling somehow ashamed of being Japanese. And Yuki hated that.

Yuki didn't want to talk to Mrs. Henley now or answer any more of her silly questions. She marched straight toward their mailbox and found two letters inside. She told Mrs. Henley she had homework to do, and she rushed upstairs to their apartment two steps at a time. She didn't even look at the letters until she was alone upstairs. She felt like Pepper taking his bone behind his house, waiting until no one was around to enjoy it. Some things needed to be savored in private without curious eyes watching.

Once she was upstairs, Yuki took the letters to the window seat where the afternoon sun filtered through the gold-leafed maple, making lacy patterns that danced over the cushions.

The first letter was for Mama and Papa from their old friend, Mr. Toda, who seemed almost like a grandfather to her. He'd gone with them on their Sunday picnics and eaten holiday dinners with them and come often just to talk to Mama and Papa over a cup of tea. Whenever he came, he never forgot to bring something for Yuki. Sometimes it was a crisp white bag filled with jelly beans or fruit drops oozing with pink juices. Sometimes it was just a package of gum. He didn't quite know how to talk to her, so instead he had brought her the small child gifts that always pleased her. Now he was still in Topaz, living in the camp's bachelor quarters because he had no family of his own. Yuki gave his letter a little pat and, setting it aside, eagerly opened the second one, a bulging pink envelope addressed to her from Emi.

"Dear lucky Yuki on the outside," Emi began. "Do you know what Grandma said last night? She said we were staying right here in Topaz until we're allowed back in California. She said she couldn't leave Grandpa buried all alone out in the desert, and she's not leaving until we can dig up his bones and take him back to bury him in California where he belongs."

Yuki shuddered as she remembered how Emi's grandpa had been shot by a sentry in the guard tower who thought he was trying to escape. "He was only looking for arrowheads," she murmured now, saying again the words Grandma Kurihara had cried over and over when she heard what happened.

Yuki knew Emi's grandma was strong and determined. If she had made up her mind, she'd probably never change it. Poor Emi, Yuki thought, she'd never be able to come out to Salt Lake City now.

"Know what else Grandma said?" Emi's letter went on. "She said it's too dangerous to go outside. She said the Japanese are getting beat up and shot at because a lot of people still hate us. Do they? Are you scared?"

It wasn't that Yuki was scared. It was just that she didn't feel comfortable. No matter where she went, she felt that people saw her as the enemy just because she looked Japanese. But Salt Lake City was a lot better than California. She wished she could make Grandma Kurihara understand. Even if you were scared, it was better to be free than to be kept inside a barbed wire fence. She knew Papa could find her a job if only she'd come out here.

But it had been many weeks before Papa himself had found a job. He said nobody wanted to hire an enemy alien just out of camp and one who was also paroled from a prisoner of war camp before that.

"But you didn't do anything wrong," Yuki defended Papa. "Tell them the FBI sent you to that POW camp just because you worked for a Japanese company in San Francisco. That's all."

Papa had looked bleak. "Well, that's reason enough for some people not to want me. Besides," he added, "no one seems to need an ex-manager of a Japanese shipping company."

That was why Mama had gotten a job first through their land-lady. She went to work for a rich white lady with eight children.

"Eight children!" Yuki gasped when Mama first told her.

No wonder they needed Mama to help them clean house. In fact, Mrs. Griswold had asked her to come every day to wash for them as well, but Papa wouldn't allow it. Mama had trouble with her back and Papa worried about her.

"It's bad enough you have to work at all, Mama," he said soberly. "I'm certainly not going to have you doing another family's wash."

"I'd be willing, Papa, until you find work."

But Papa wouldn't hear of it. "Your father would climb out of his grave and haunt me if I allowed you to wash the soiled garments of someone else's family."

Mama smiled faintly at the thought. "He might at that," she murmured, "even though many Japanese women have had to do it."

Yuki's grandfathers had died in Japan long before she was born. They had both been brave samurai warriors in years long past, and that was something to be proud of. It meant Yuki and her brother were the grandchildren of two samurai, so they had to be brave and courageous and loyal too. It meant being strong when necessary, but still having a gentle heart capable of loving beautiful things. It meant they had a past to live up to, and Yuki wasn't sure she could manage.

For her, Japan was an alien land she'd never seen, and her grandfathers seemed more like people she'd read about than anybody linked to her by blood. If she died and met up with them in Heaven, she might not even recognize them. She imagined them to be rather fierce-looking gentlemen, splendid in samurai armor, wearing swords at their sides and carrying bannered spears.

They'd probably take one look at her and sniff. "Who is this strange, ignorant creature who has black hair and brown eyes like ours, but speaks only the language of the foreigner?"

And Yuki would have to look down at her toes and say, "I'm Yuki Sakane, your twelve-year-old grandchild, but I didn't go to Japanese language school to study Japanese like Mama wanted me to."

Sometimes Yuki looked at herself and thought it strange that she looked so Japanese when she didn't feel very Japanese inside. Her black hair had no trace of a wave or curl. Her brown eyes were not as wide as Emi's nor double-lidded as Mama's were. She was just an ordinary, round-faced Nisei born in California but neither totally American nor totally Japanese.

Eventually Papa found a job as a shipping clerk in a department store downtown. He had been pushed back to doing the kind of work he might have done when he first arrived from Japan. It was as though he'd suddenly lost almost thirty years of his life and work.

But Papa only said, "*Shikata ga nai.* It can't be helped. Some people have lost everything, and young men are losing their lives in this war. At least I'm alive and healthy and that's something to be thankful for."

Mama felt bad that Papa had to be a shipping clerk when he had the brains and experience to be the manager of the store. And Papa felt bad that Mama had to be somebody's cleaning woman when she should have been at home growing flowers and writing poetry and not straining her back. But that's the way things were and there was no changing them.

Yuki hurried through the rest of Emi's seven-page letter and came to the last paragraph.

"Try hard to think of a way we can get Grandma to go out to Salt Lake City," she wrote. "And please answer immediately. I WANT TO GET OUT!!! Desperately yours, Emi."

Chapter 3

"YUKI, I'm home." It was Mama.

"We got some mail," Yuki shouted as soon as she heard her mother coming up the stairs.

"From your brother?"

"No, but two letters from Topaz. Mama, how can we make Emi's grandma come out of camp?"

Mama sighed, trying to hide her disappointment at not hearing from Ken.

"Yuki, we can't make her do anything she doesn't want to do." Mama understood how Grandma Kurihara felt about leaving her husband behind buried all alone in the desert. "You've got to wait until she's ready," she said softly.

"Oh gloom," Yuki muttered. "She won't be ready until the war ends and that might not be for another ten years."

Mama wasn't listening. She had put on her glasses and was reading Mr. Toda's letter, the wrinkles gathering around her eyes in a slow, easy smile.

"Mr. Toda sent me one of his poems," she explained.

Old Mr. Toda had never written a poem in his entire life, until he was sent to camp. Then it was as though all his lonely longing came tumbling out, caught now in the delicate web of poetry.

"Read it to me," Yuki said.

But when Mama began to read aloud, it was as though Yuki were listening to a bagful of sounds that made no sense. She couldn't understand the poetic Japanese words.

It was the same when Yuki listened to the poems Mama scribbled on a scrap of paper or the edge of a newspaper. Mama tried to explain them to her, but it was like trying to describe the smell of a rose. The poems were Mama's secret other self, a shadowy presence, and Yuki could only guess at understanding the things Mama felt deep inside and couldn't tell anyone, not even Papa.

What Papa wrote were things like business letters and checks. He also kept a ledger of their household accounts with neat columns of figures that had their own special meaning for him. He took care of all the bills because he said if he left that to

Mama, she'd probably write poetry on the back of the bills and forget all about paying them.

But Yuki knew Papa was proud of Mama's poems. He told her to send them to the Japanese newspaper and try to get them published.

"Well, maybe . . . someday," was all Mama would say, however, and she never even copied her poems on a clean sheet of paper. It was as though she felt that for now she should keep her poetry on the outer fringes of her life.

Yuki waited for Mama to tell her what Mr. Toda had written, but all she said was, "I wish we had room here for Mr. Toda and could get him out of camp." She was silent for a few minutes and then said, "Well, someday Mr. Toda will be free, and so will Emi and her grandma. We just have to be patient."

"I wish this darn war would hurry up and end so we can all go back to California," Yuki said wistfully. "Then everything will be perfect again."

Mama looked thoughtful. "I hope so, Yuki," she said. "I surely hope so."

She stood up then and put on her apron. "I'm making one of Papa's favorites tonight—fried noodles with pork."

"How come? Is it a special day?"

"No, I just thought he might need some cheering up today," Mama answered vaguely and disappeared into the kitchen.

Yuki didn't have time to wonder why. If she hurried, she'd just have time to write Emi a quick note before Papa came home.

Nov. 3, 1944

Miss Emi Kurihara
Block 7, Barrack 5, Room 2-a
Topaz, Utah
Dearest Emi:

Here I am answering your letter immediately, just like you told me to. I think your grandma's crazy to want to stay in camp, but Mama says we can't make her come out if she doesn't want to. Besides, I guess she wouldn't want to be anybody's cleaning lady out here in Salt Lake City anyway.

Yuki grinned at the mere thought of anybody telling Grandma Kurihara what to do. If anybody was giving orders, it would have to be Emi's grandma. She liked being in charge of things, the way she was when she had her own grocery store in San

Francisco. It wasn't that she was always bossy and stubborn. There was probably a gathering of gentle thoughts somewhere inside the old woman, Yuki thought, but she wasn't like Mama. She could seldom show them to anyone. Not even to Emi.

"Well, never mind," Yuki continued. "One of these days . . ."

She had to stop, for she heard Papa coming in downstairs.

"*Tadaima*, I'm home," he called.

The wonderful smell of fried pork and onions was drifting through their apartment and down the steps to welcome him, but instead of remarking how good supper smelled, Papa slumped wearily into his big armchair.

"Wretched creature," he muttered.

"Who—me, Papa?"

"No, no, Yuki. Of course not you."

Mama came from the kitchen still holding her long cooking chopsticks. "How did it go today, Papa?" she asked.

"More of the same," Papa answered with a long sigh.

Then Yuki remembered. It was the day of the month Papa had to report to the parole officer at the Immigration Board. She still felt a stab of anger when she recalled how the three FBI men had taken Papa away like a common criminal. But he had been one of the lucky ones, released early to join them in Topaz. Now that he was out of camp, however, he had to report to a parole officer each month and would have to until the war ended.

"What'd he want to know today?" Yuki asked.

"He asked in which direction I would shoot if I had a gun and was standing between American and Japanese soldiers."

"*Mah!*" Mama was flabbergasted.

"So what'd you say, Papa?"

Papa took off his glasses and rubbed his eyes. The question was so ridiculous, he began now to smile at the thought of it.

"What could I say?" he asked with a shrug. "I told him I'd point the gun straight up and shoot at the sun."

"And then what'd he say?"

"He made me fill out the same fifteen-page questionnaire all over again."

No wonder Papa was in a bad mood. But his black moods never lasted long, and already his anger was melting away. "I suppose the poor fool only thought he was doing his job."

"Well, it's over until next month," Mama comforted. "Now come and enjoy your fried noodles. You'll feel better."

Papa got up and started toward the kitchen. But before he

left the living room, Yuki saw him take the evening newspaper from his coat pocket and stuff it quickly into the wastepaper basket. That was strange because Papa never threw out a paper until it was at least a day old. Was there something in the paper that Papa didn't want them to see? Yuki intended to find out as soon as supper was over.

Chapter 4

AS soon as she could, Yuki retrieved Papa's newspaper from the wastepaper basket and took it to her room. She found the article about the 442nd RCT and now she knew why Papa had hidden it from Mama.

The 442 had been sent to France and was in a terrible, bloody battle in the forests of the Vosges Mountains trying to rescue a battalion cut off from water, food, and medical supplies. The words "withering enemy fire" kept echoing in her mind as Yuki read about the steep, rugged mountain forest dotted with mines, and the artillery shells exploding against the trees and showering the men with shrapnel.

Yuki felt weak in the knees just thinking of Ken in the midst of all that terror. And when she went to sleep that night, her nightmares shifted from the dust storms of Topaz to the battle in the Vosges Mountains.

It was raining and cold, and somehow Yuki was over there with Ken, struggling up a slippery mountain path, with a full pack on her back and an M-1 rifle in her hand. She could hear the German shells coming closer and closer as she slogged through miles of mud, watching closely not to step on a mine. Her bones ached, her eyes burned from lack of sleep, and she could feel the cold rain seeping through her clothes, wet and damp against her skin.

She was trying hard to catch up with Ken, but he was "going for broke," giving everything he had, trying to prove he was a good American. And he wouldn't wait for her.

"Ken!" she shouted, but he never turned around, and soon he disappeared entirely into the mountain mists.

"Ken!" she called out a second desperate time. Then she woke up shivering.

What did soldiers do when it rained, Yuki wondered. How did they ever get their socks dry? Suppose all Ken had was a cold, muddy foxhole to jump into, with water puddling up all around, his boots and socks soaked through? Suppose Ken got killed before he could ever have a nice hot meal or sleep again in a warm, dry bed? Yuki couldn't bear even to think about it.

"Kenichi Sakane," she murmured. "You'd just better not get yourself killed over there, or I'll never ever forgive you."

The next evening Yuki broke Mama's best crystal bud vase. Mama had wrapped it up in her gray wool sweater and carried it with her all the way from Berkeley to Topaz in the desert, and finally to Salt Lake City. It was a special vase she used when she put a flower beside the photographs of Yuki's grandparents on the anniversary day of their death. It was the vase she used too for Hana, the older sister Yuki had never seen, who had died when she was only one year old and was buried in the cemetery in the hills of Oakland.

Mama never talked about Hana, but she always kept a snapshot of her on the bureau. It was turning brown now, but the silver frame it was in was always polished and shiny. It would have been nice, Yuki sometimes thought, to have a sister who'd always be there to do things with.

The day before they had to leave Berkeley and go to the concentration camp, Mama had gone to the cemetery to say goodbye to Hana. She took her a bouquet of all the flowers she could gather from their garden and told her not to worry. She told her Papa was in a prisoner of war camp and the rest of them were about to be sent to another kind of camp, but they'd all be back when the war was over, and for her to rest in peace until then. She had pulled out the weeds around the small gray tombstone and then watered one last time the flowering cherry tree she and Papa had planted there.

And now Yuki had broken Mama's crystal vase and she'd never have it again to put beside Hana's picture, or anybody else's. It had slipped through her soapy fingers just as she was putting it on the dish rack and crashed to the floor in a mass of sharp, jagged pieces.

Yuki felt so awful she wanted to cry. She usually didn't cry when she'd done something stupid. Sometimes she just tried to cover it up by acting as though it weren't important. Another time she might have swept up the pieces before Mama saw them and used her own money to buy her another bud vase.

But tonight it was different. She knew how much the vase meant to Mama, and she also had this terrible feeling that it was a bad omen. It meant something had happened to Ken. She just knew it. All day she'd had these anxious feelings about Ken and now she knew why. Something had happened to him, and maybe she'd never see him again.

"Oh, Mama," Yuki wailed.

Mama put her arms around her and held her close. "That's all right, Yuki," she said. "It was an accident."

And then as though she knew exactly what Yuki was thinking, she said, "Look at it this way, Yuki. Maybe my vase was broken in order to spare your brother. Maybe it was destroyed in place of something happening to Ken."

Mama smiled a sort of half-smile, as though she were remembering something from long ago. "That's what your grandma would have said, Yuki. She used to say that objects sometimes have lives of their own and that sometimes they die in order to spare us."

Yuki knew Mama was trying to make her feel better. Mama swept up the broken pieces of glass and put them in a newspaper. She folded the newspaper neatly and carefully, almost as though it were a gift. Then she laid it gently in the garbage can, giving the vase a sort of burial rather than just dumping it out unceremoniously.

"There," she said, brushing her hands. "Now I think I'll write a letter to your brother."

Mama had already written him two letters that week, but they hadn't had a letter from Ken in over a month.

"No news is good news," Papa said.

But suppose Ken were wounded, Yuki thought, and his company had moved on without him. Suppose nobody found him and he was lying there in the rain, bleeding to death and . . .

Yuki felt a sharp sadness that surfaced into a sob.

She found one more piece of glass that Mama had missed and dropped it carefully into the trash can. She almost felt as though she'd killed Ken herself.

Chapter 5

CHRISTMAS had seemed sad and empty this year because for the first time in her life Yuki didn't have any close friends to share it with.

Mama did her best to bring the Christmas spirit into their apartment. She bought a small crèche at the five and ten cents store and put it up on the table in the living room.

Mary and Joseph and the baby Jesus were there, surrounded by the animals of the barnyard and the shepherds and the three wisemen with their gifts. It was beautiful and peaceful, as though Bethlehem were right there in their living room.

"Maybe the world has gone crazy," Mama said, "but the Christmas story is still the same. It's important to remember that, Yuki, and not forget what Christmas really means."

"Uh-huh."

Yuki understood. But she couldn't help wishing things were different.

"Don't keep wishing for what can't be," Papa told her. "Be happy for this special Christmas we have now."

But Yuki thought of the Christmases back home in Berkeley when the house was filled with the tantalizing smell of Mama's cookies baking in the oven and the glorious fresh green smell of the Christmas tree by the front window. This year Mama was too busy to do all the things she used to do back home.

Yuki remembered the Christmas Eves when she delivered Mama's cookies to the neighbors, and Mrs. Jamieson would ask her to stay for a cup of sweet, creamy cocoa.

Then there was the Christmas program at their small Japanese church, all decorated with red and green paper streamers and bells, and a giant Christmas tree with enormous colored balls and silver tinsel. The church was always crowded on Christmas Eve when the Sunday School put on its program.

Yuki remembered how cold it was in the drafty parsonage parlor where they changed into their costumes for the nativity scene, squealing and shivering around the small gas heater as they shook off their heavy coats and new Christmas clothes. Yuki was usually one of the angels, dressed in scratchy white gauze with a silver halo that slithered down on her forehead. She giggled and whispered with her friends until it was time to appear on stage. But once she was in her place and the choir sang "O Holy Night," somehow the special feeling of Christmas wrapped her up like a comforting blanket on a cold, foggy night.

Afterwards, Mama and Papa's friends gathered around, telling her in their soft Japanese voices how beautiful the program had been. Maybe that was part of it, Yuki thought now. She missed her own friends, but she missed Mama and Papa's friends too, with their Japanese talk and their genial bows and even the smelly yellow pickles they brought to picnics. Maybe that's what was wrong with this Christmas. Here in Salt Lake City their world was made up only of *hakujin*—white people who were strangers to them in a strange city that wasn't home.

The doorbell suddenly jangled Yuki out of her dreams. Papa was at work and Mama had ventured out, though it was snowing hard, bundled up in her warmest coat and scarf, to buy groceries. "We have to eat," she'd said, "snowstorm or not."

Yuki ran down the steps, saw a shadowy person on the other side of the lace-covered glass of the front door, and wondered who it could be. When she opened the door, she saw it was a boy with a telegram, and she wanted to slam the door shut and pretend he had never come. She had an awful feeling he'd brought terrible news about Ken. She'd known something had happened to him from the moment she'd broken Mama's crystal bud vase.

Mrs. Henley was just coming up the front steps, trudging heavily in her boots and her shabby fur coat with its frayed cuffs where the leather was beginning to show. She saw what Yuki held in her hand.

"It's not bad news is it, Yuki?" she asked.

"I . . . I don't know."

"Is your mama home?"

Yuki shook her head. "She's gone to the market."

Mrs. Henley's face was red from the wind and her breath came in short gasps that left wisps of steam in the brittle, cold air.

Yuki was surprised by the gentleness in her voice. "Don't fret now, my dear," she said softly. "Do you want me to open it for you?"

Yuki nodded. Her throat was tight and dry, and her heart felt as though it might explode. She couldn't talk and she could scarcely think. She was glad to hand the envelope to Mrs. Henley, as though by giving it to her she could be rid of the awful news inside.

Mrs. Henley pulled off her damp gloves and ripped open the envelope. And then she smiled. "Why, Yuki, it's all right," she said brightly. "Your brother's only been wounded. He's been evacuated to a hospital, but he's all right. Maybe he'll even be sent home soon."

Then for the first time she gave Yuki a warm, loving hug, and Yuki hugged her back.

It was funny how the telegram about Ken made them all so happy. Here poor Ken was lying in some hospital with shrapnel wounds in his leg, but Mama and Papa and Yuki were overjoyed because Ken hadn't been killed.

"It's all right now, Mama," Papa said over and over again. "Ken is alive."

And Mama couldn't stop crying because she was so relieved. None of them had dared speak aloud what each feared, but Yuki knew she wasn't the only one who had feared the worst.

"Mrs. Henley said maybe he'd get sent home soon," Yuki said hopefully.

"Oh I do hope so," Mama answered. "I can't believe he's really all right until I see him with my own eyes." Then she said something else.

"You know, good things often happen in threes. Maybe two more nice things will happen before long."

As usual, Mama was right. A few weeks later, Papa heard that the army had revoked the exclusion order against the Japanese on the West Coast.

Yuki had never seen him so excited in a long time.

"Do you know what that means?" he asked, pacing back and forth in the living room because he couldn't sit still.

"It means we can go back to California now if we want to. It means we can go home to Berkeley. The army can't keep us out any more."

Yuki leaped from her chair and hung on Papa's neck as she used to do when she was little.

"Can we go home then, Papa? Can we go back to Berkeley?"

"I don't see why not," Papa answered quickly. "I'm sure I can find a sponsor there to vouch for me."

"But where will we live?" Mama wondered. "Our old house is rented now to someone else."

"We'll find something," Papa assured her. "Don't worry. We'll find a way." And he went straight to the desk and began writing some letters.

It was a while before the third good thing happened, but it finally did. The Reverend Wada wrote to Papa that he'd gotten permission to leave Camp Topaz and was going back to their Japanese church in Berkeley.

"My wife and I will open our church again and turn it into a hostel so the returning Japanese will have a place to stay until they can find proper housing," he wrote. "Won't you and your family join us as soon as possible and help us open up our church once more? I will secure a sponsor for you, Mr. Sakane, and do whatever is necessary to facilitate your return."

Now they had a place to go and California could no longer keep them out.

"Start packing, Mama," Papa said as soon as he read the Reverend Wada's letter. "We're going home."

Chapter 6

YUKI had never thought she'd feel sad about leaving Salt Lake City and saying good-bye to Mr. and Mrs. Henley, but she did, just a little. Each time she had to say good-bye to someone, it was as though she were leaving behind a small piece of herself. She'd already had so many partings since the war began, from her friends in Berkeley, then from Ken, and last year from her friends in Topaz. If she had to say many more farewells, she felt as though there'd soon be nothing left of her old self.

When Yuki said so to Mama, she got one of those thoughtful looks that came over her face when she had an idea for a poem.

"That's all right, Yuki," she said. "It's nice to leave a bit of ourselves with our friends, isn't it? Then we go on to new things and new places, and maybe we become different and more interesting people."

Yuki hadn't thought of it like that. Maybe she was already so different Mrs. Jamieson or Mimi Nelson wouldn't even know her when she got back to Berkeley. She'd grown two inches and gained six pounds from all the beans and potatoes and bread she'd eaten in camp. And she knew her face looked different. The desert sun and wind had tanned it to the color of dark toast, and the long months in the desert had left her with a bleak, lonely look.

On the morning they were to leave Salt Lake City, Mrs. Henley came upstairs with a box of sandwiches and fruit and cookies for them to eat on the train.

"Come back and visit us someday when the war is over," she said to Yuki.

"Okay, Mrs. Henley," Yuki said. But deep in her heart she knew she didn't mean it. She didn't ever want to come back to Utah again. For her Utah would always mean Topaz, the concentration camp in the desert. It would mean the choking dust storms and the place where Emi's grandfather was shot to death, leaving Emi with no one else in the world except her grandma. But she gave Mrs. Henley a small hug and thanked her for the lunch to eat on the train.

A cold shiver of nervous excitement surged through her as Yuki waited with Mama and Papa for their train to glide into the crowded station. She felt jumpy and a little scared, like the time they were released from camp and came outside. Yuki carried a bulging shopping bag stuffed with the last-minute things she couldn't squeeze into her suitcase, and she tried hard to be small and quiet and inconspicuous so no one would notice her or hate her for being Japanese. When the train came in, it was crowded with soldiers on leave and with women and children going to see their husbands and fathers in military camps. Yuki knew some of the soldiers were on their way to the Pacific to join the battle against Japan.

She stayed close to Mama and Papa, following them quickly to their seats in the crowded coach. She was relieved to see that the chairs were soft and comfortable and not like the stiff, hard seats they'd sat on for three days when they rode the train out to Utah.

"Look, Mama, the seats lean back," Yuki said, testing her own chair. But Mama quickly warned her to push her chair back up. "You mustn't bother the people behind us," she said firmly. "You mustn't make a nuisance of yourself."

They had to be careful not to annoy anybody. But even if Yuki did nothing, there were some people who became angry anyway. It happened the first night when Yuki went to the restroom at the rear of their coach. Just as she opened the door to go in, a blond woman with two small children pushed past her. She glared angrily at Yuki and muttered, "Go back where you belong, you damn Jap."

She said it in such a low voice, at first Yuki couldn't believe she'd actually heard the words. But when she saw the look of hate on the woman's face, she knew the woman had not only said it, she'd really meant it.

Yuki felt as though she'd been kicked in the stomach. She felt so awful she couldn't even tell Mama about it when she went back to her seat. It seemed somehow shameful to repeat the horrible words, as though by saying them again she would spread more filth on herself and on Mama as well.

After that, Yuki never went back to use the restroom in their coach. Instead, she walked two cars forward to use another one and often she asked Mama to go with her. Mama never asked her why, she just went with her. Maybe Mama knew without Yuki's telling her what had happened. Maybe the blond woman had spat her hateful words at Mama too.

As the train made its way westward through wide plains and deserts and small, sleepy towns, Yuki felt as though it would never get to California.

"I can't stand being on this train another minute," she complained to Mama.

But Mama reminded her how much nicer this was than the long train ride going in the other direction. Of course she was

right. On the train to Topaz, there had been car captains assigned to each coach. They saw to it that the shades were kept
drawn from sunset to sunrise and that no one left his car to go
to another except twice a day at specified times. They had been
allowed to get off the train only once during the three-day trip,
and that was for ten minutes in the middle of a Nevada desert
while armed soldiers stood guard so no one would try to escape.

This time they were free to do whatever they wished. Yuki got
off and ran around at every station where the train stopped,
rushing to the small stands to buy magazines and orange pop
and candy bars and peanuts.

The last morning was the longest of all. "Papa, are we almost
there?"

"The conductor said we were two hours late, Yuki. It'll probably be close to three o'clock by the time we get to Berkeley."

Three o'clock! Yuki had been awake since six that morning,
partly because all her bones ached from sitting for so long, but
mostly because she was so excited at the thought of finally
reaching California.

"Who do you think will be there to meet us, Mama?"

"Why Reverend Wada, I expect."

"Anybody else?"

Mama knew Yuki had written to Mrs. Jamieson and Mimi
telling them of their arrival on the "City of San Francisco."

"Don't count on anybody else," Mama cautioned. "You know
Mrs. Jamieson is lame, and with Mimi's mama working at the
defense plant now, you mustn't expect Mimi either."

"Uh-huh."

Yuki knew all that as well as Mama. Still, she couldn't help
hoping somebody besides the Reverend Wada would be there so
it would seem like a real homecoming.

It was impossible for Yuki to sit still until three o'clock. She
couldn't concentrate on any of the books in her shopping bag.
She got tired of looking out the window. She chewed two packages of Juicy Fruit gum and ate three small bags of salted
peanuts. Then she had to climb over Mama so many times to go
for a drink of water that Mama finally made her sit in the aisle
seat. After a while, Yuki changed places with Papa, so he could
sit with Mama and she sat in the aisle seat across from them.

At last, when she thought she couldn't bear another minute
on the train, Yuki saw the smoky old brick buildings of Crock-
ett, close to the waters of Carquinez Strait, and she knew they
were almost there. It wouldn't be long now. She watched eagerly

for the first glimpse of San Francisco Bay and then for the buildings of Berkeley edged up to the water and spreading back into the hills to the east.

At last the conductor called out, "Next stop, Berkeley. This way out." The train began to slow down, slipping past wigwagging signs blinking and clanging to hold back the cars. Then Yuki saw the round cream-colored dome of the depot with its "Berkeley" sign, and she could no longer contain herself.

"Mama! Papa! We're here!" she shouted. And without waiting for them, she ran ahead and was the first person to get off the train.

Almost immediately she saw the Reverend Wada, dressed up in his best black suit, waving a shabby felt hat. Yuki waved back, and then turned to urge Mama and Papa to hurry. When she looked again, she saw the green coat and the fluff of red hair under an enormous green hat.

"Mrs. Jamieson!" Yuki shouted, running toward her. "You came! You came!"

Mrs. Jamieson wrapped her up in a warm hug that smelled of lavender and cloves. "You didn't think I'd let you come home and not find me here to greet you, did you? I've been reminding Reverend Wada every day for the past week to bring me along to the station."

Yuki looked around. "Did Mimi come?"

"She couldn't come, Yuki, but she sent her love. So did her mama and papa."

"Oh. Well, never mind."

"The important thing is that you're back at last," Mrs. Jamieson reminded her.

And of course she was right. That was all that really mattered, and coming home to Mrs. Jamieson was all the welcome Yuki needed, at least for now.

Chapter 7

IT seemed strange being back in Berkeley and yet not being able to go to their old house. They could only look at it from across the street when they dropped off Mrs. Jamieson.

"It just hasn't been the same since you left," she murmured as she struggled out of the car. "I hardly know the new family there."

Yuki looked at the neat stucco bungalow with the wide front porch where she had often sat with Pepper on a long summer's day. "Maybe someday those people will move and then we can rent it again and everything'll be like it was," she said hopefully.

But no one was listening to her. Mama was peering out the car window trying to see how the garden looked. "The camellias aren't blooming," she observed quietly." And neither is the wisteria. Shouldn't they be in bloom by now, Papa?"

Papa didn't seem to want to see what had become of their beautiful garden. "Nothing stays the same, Mama," he pointed out. "You'll only be disappointed if you think nothing ever changes."

Although he spoke to Mama, it was Yuki he was looking at. It was as though he wanted her to understand something he'd already learned himself.

But Papa's wrong, Yuki thought. Mrs. Jamieson hadn't changed at all. She was every bit as nice as she'd always been, and Yuki loved her just as much. Before she could say so, however, the Reverend Wada lifted his hat and started up the engine.

"See you soon, Mrs. Jamieson," Yuki called. And they were on their way to the Japanese church.

"I hope you aren't expecting too much," the Reverend Wada said a bit apologetically. "The old house behind the church that we always used for a student dormitory is in pretty bad shape. It needs a lot of cleaning before we can use it as a hostel."

"But there is a place for us to sleep tonight?" Papa asked cautiously.

"Oh yes, don't worry." The Reverend Wada waved a thin hand to brush aside Papa's concerns. "Everything is arranged. We've borrowed some cots and put them in the chapel and the parsonage and . . . well, you'll soon see."

Now the car pulled into the graveled driveway beside the church. Yuki thought it still looked almost the same, with its tall bell tower that had a cross, but never had had a bell. Yet it seemed shabbier and somehow battered, with gray streaks running down the sides of the building and paper patches on its cracked windows.

Mrs. Wada hurried from the parsonage to greet them, with her three small children swarming around her. They surrounded Yuki, pulling at her coat, wanting her to see where they were all going to sleep that night.

"Come look," they urged in high, excited voices. "We're going to sleep with the organ."

Yuki let herself be pulled inside the church and turned toward the dim, high-ceilinged chapel. The last of the afternoon sun filtered through the tall, arched windows, giving the dark wood paneling a warm, earthy glow. It seemed strange to see the chapel empty, without the usual clusters of people sitting in the pews, the dark-suited men on the left of the center aisle and the women, in their Sunday hats and coats, sitting on the right.

It felt odd not to see the Reverend Wada standing at the pulpit in his black morning coat, raising his voice so it reached out to the very last row. It always surprised Yuki that such a large voice could come from such a frail man.

The children clattered nosily down the center aisle to the back of the chapel, looking to see if Yuki was following. Then they raced up the steps to the small balcony that held the church organ.

"Look," they said, grinning with pleasure. "Here's where we sleep tonight."

In the far corner of the balcony, Yuki saw the old reed organ with its faded green foot pedals. It was covered up with a wrinkled sheet, and in front of it were six army cots lined up as though they were in a tent at summer camp.

"Am I sleeping up here too?" Yuki asked.

The children nodded. "You're taking care of us."

"Oh. And where do my mama and papa sleep?"

"In our room in the parsonage."

Yuki swallowed the knot of disappointment that welled up inside her. This wasn't exactly what she'd expected.

"Well, you knew you were staying at the church, didn't you?" she asked herself. "You knew it was a hostel now. You knew you couldn't go back to the old house across from Mrs. Jamieson's."

Yes, she knew all that. Still, there was something lonely and sad about the musty, empty church that had been used by strangers while they were in camp. She'd expected to feel happier at being back.

As soon as the three Wada children calmed down and went to sleep that night, Yuki composed a letter to Emi in her head.

"It feels weird sleeping here in the empty church with the old organ covered up like a big white ghost and three kids sound asleep next to me," she began.

Then she decided the situation called for something more direct. "Hurry up and come back before somebody else takes the two empty cots next to mine," she said, sending one of her mental messages. "You too, Mr. Toda," she continued. "Hurry on back." And Ken. What should she say to Ken?

Before she had decided, she fell asleep, and the next thing she knew, something had leaped on her stomach and was walking slowly toward her neck.

"Eeeee! Help!" Yuki let out a terrible screech and wondered if she were having another nightmare. She sat bolt upright on her cot and discovered it was already morning. The sun was streaming into the balcony from the circular window behind her. The three Wada children were gone, their beds empty and unmade. And the horrible creature that had given her such a scare was only a striped alley cat.

Yuki didn't like cats. "Scat! Shoo! Get out!" She jumped on her cot and threw her pillow at the cat. With a startled yowl, it leaped away and scampered toward the organ where it disappeared beneath the sheet.

"Here now! That's no way to treat my cat!"

Yuki turned to see a short, heavy-set man with wild, bushy gray hair that looked a little like a bird's nest. His steel-rimmed spectacles were halfway down his nose, and he wore a pair of rumpled trousers and a shirt that needed mending. He gave her a disapproving look.

"Hokusai was only being friendly," he said dourly. "He's a fine cat, and he's named after a famous Japanese artist. But I suppose you wouldn't know about things like that."

Yuki slid quickly back under the covers and pulled them up to her nose. "I don't like cats," she said firmly. And then, so she wouldn't sound too mean, she added, "But I love dogs."

The old man made no comment. He was on his hands and knees crawling around the dusty floor, trying to find his cat. "Come, Hokusai," he called. "*Sah, oide, oide.* Pay no attention to this cross young lady."

"I'm not a cross . . ." Yuki began.

But now the old man took a piece of dried fish from his pocket and held it out for the cat. "Come, Hokusai. Come."

Quickly the cat emerged from under the sheet, flicked its tail and rubbed gently against the old man's legs before it nibbled at the fish.

"There, you see," the old man said. "I told you he was a fine cat. Maybe he'll even get to like you someday."

Then he picked up his cat in the crook of his arm and, speaking softly to it in Japanese, he clattered noisily down the stairs.

Yuki didn't see the old man again until that night at supper, but she did see his cat roaming around the parsonage.

"I'm sorry about throwing that pillow at you," she said to it. "I guess you can't help it if you're a cat."

Hokusai looked at her for a long time, whiskers twitching, yellow eyes staring, and then stalked off with an imperial air, and Yuki didn't know if she'd been forgiven or not.

Mama helped Mrs. Wada cook a good supper of rice and stew that evening, with plenty of pickled cabbage to eat at the end of the meal. Yuki saw the old man take two helpings of everything, and then lean back in his chair to enjoy a cigarette.

Papa talked to him as though he were an old friend. "Well, Mr. Oka," he said, "tell us what luck you had today. Were you able to make arrangements to buy back your grocery store?"

A frown quickly swept over the old man's face. "Miller won't sell my Sunshine Grocery back to me unless I pay him five thousand dollars cash and take over the lease." The old man took a quick puff of his cigarette and added, "Do you know what he paid me for the shop when I was forced to sell it to him and go to camp?"

"Probably not much," Papa guessed.

"All of four hundred dollars, for the stock on my shelves, all the fixtures, and the good will I'd built up in the neighborhood for ten years."

The old man scowled and drew in a noisy gulp of tea. He shook his head sadly. "Scoundrels," he muttered darkly. "They're all scoundrels."

Mama knew what Mr. Oka was thinking. "Not all, Mr. Oka. Not all," she said quickly and went to the kitchen to return with a two-layer chocolate cake dripping with thick frosting and sprinkled with nuts.

"Look what our friend, Mrs. Jamieson, sent over to us today. She said it was to welcome us all back. That includes you too, Mr. Oka."

"And on Saturday ten students from the campus church are coming to help us paint the old dormitory in back," the Reverend Wada added.

"Cake and paint are all fine and good," Mr. Oka admitted, "but what I need now is some cash to buy back my old Sunshine Grocery, and who's going to give me that? Who can give me back the business I lost?"

Papa looked thoughtful. "Maybe we can find a way to help you, Mr. Oka," he said slowly. "We're all going to have to work together to get back on our feet again."

Yuki wondered how Papa was ever going to help the old man

when he had no job himself. The Japanese shipping company he worked for no longer existed and he needed to find a house for them to rent too. Papa certainly had a lot to do before he could help Mr. Oka.

"Papa," Yuki began, when she felt something nudge her foot. Then she felt a soft, furry body sweep past her legs. She looked down and let out such a scream that Mama dropped her teacup and spilled tea all over the table.

"It's a dead mouse!" Yuki shouted, at which point, everybody rose very quickly from the table. But Mr. Oka came to pick up the small gray mouse by the tail.

"Well, well," he said, looking pleased. "Hokusai has brought you one of his gifts. I guess he's forgiven you, in spite of the way you treated him this morning."

When he'd disposed of the mouse, he returned saying, "If Hokusai says you're a friend, then I guess I accept you as well." And thrusting a rough, calloused hand at Yuki, he shook her hand solemnly with a firm, hard grip.

Yuki wasn't sure why, but it seemed important to be considered his friend.

"Thanks, Mr. Oka," she said. "Thanks a lot."

Chapter 8

"YOU can have one of the second floor rooms in the back dormitory if you're willing to clean it up," the Reverend Wada told Yuki the next morning.

"I'm willing! I'm willing!" Yuki answered eagerly.

She was longing to have a room of her own where she could put in two extra cots for Emi and her grandma. Papa had already guaranteed a home for them and Mr. Toda when they returned, and he'd also made sure Mrs. Kurihara could bring her husband's remains back with her.

Cleaning up the old dormitory was much more work than Yuki thought it would be. Even Papa and the Reverend Wada were discouraged by the dirt and junk left by war workers who had lived in the house while the Japanese were away. The roomers hadn't cared much about the house, because for them it was only a place to spend a few months and then move on.

Yuki looked around her room now, wondering if maybe this was the very room where old Mr. Toda had once lived long ago when the house first became a dormitory for the young men from

Japan. He had often told her how it was in those early days, and she tried now to think of Mr. Toda as he might have been then, his hair still black, his back straight and his legs strong.

Maybe it was from this very room he had gone to clean windows or scrub floors or wash dishes in some dingy cafe, or, in the season of the summer fruit, he'd gone to the valleys to pick peaches and cherries and apricots in the scorching sun with the other young men.

Mr. Toda had told her how, when the rains came, they returned to this house and it was here waiting for them, a refuge in lonely times when they longed for a friendly Japanese face or a bowl of hot bean paste soup. Over the years most of the men had sent to Japan for wives and moved away. But Mr. Toda hadn't. Like a bird that never left its first nest, he had stayed, perhaps in this very room, Yuki thought, until the army had sent him off to the desert in Utah.

Yuki wrinkled her nose as she looked at the walls streaked by leaking rain and spattered with grease behind the small table ringed with burn marks.

Limp, ragged curtains hid the dirty window panes and a green window shade lay askew on the floor, exactly where it had fallen. Dust balls stirred lazily as Yuki walked around the room, and dust covered the cardboard cartons full of empty cans, beer bottles and food cartons encrusted still with bits of gray-green mold.

"Ugh!" Yuki sniffed.

For a minute even the church balcony with the Wada children seemed better than this mess. But when she thought of Emi and her grandma, she knew the room had to be cleaned. She took a deep breath, held it as long as she could and began to sweep the floor, flinging the dust out into the small, dark hallway.

"*Kora, kora!* Don't sweep all your dust into my room!" Mr. Oka called from the room across the hall.

"Oh, I'm sorry. I didn't know anyone else was living up here."

"Well, it was either here of join the children's brigade in the church balcony, and you wouldn't have wanted me and Hokusai up there, would you?"

"Oh no," Yuki blurted out before she realized how unfriendly that sounded. But the old man hadn't noticed.

"My room's filthy," she explained.

The old man swept past her to see for himself. "Hmmpf," he grunted. "You just need to get rid of all this junk."

And without waiting to be asked, he gathered up an armful of cartons and carted them down the steep steps, while Yuki ran after him picking up the cans and bottles he dropped along the way.

Back upstairs, Mr. Oka poured a generous amount of disinfectant into a bucket of hot soapy water and gave Yuki one of the rags he'd wrung out in it.

"The only way to get a room clean," he instructed, "is to start scrubbing. Now let's get to work. I wasn't a houseboy for twenty years for nothing."

"I thought you owned a grocery store," Yuki interrupted.

"I did. But how do you think I saved enough money to buy it in the first place?"

The old man held up his arms and flexed his muscles. "I scrubbed floors and windows like everybody else. I did it in Chicago too when I first got out of camp."

The old man stopped to light a cigarette and then grinned as though he were enjoying a small private joke of his own.

"I swore I'd never scrub another floor for anybody once I got back to California," he said, "and now look at me!"

Yuki didn't know what to say. But the old man went right on as though he were talking to himself.

Then he turned to look at her. "That's all right, little one," he said, blowing a cloud of smoke into the room. "Don't worry. This time I'm doing it because I want to. And that makes a big difference. You can call me Uncle Oka, if you like."

Yuki grinned back at him. "Okay, Uncle Oka." She still didn't quite understand this brusque old man, but she was beginning to like him.

It was the sound of a car driving into the yard and honking wildly that brought them all running outside. Papa first, then Mama and Mrs. Wada, wiping their hands on their aprons, Yuki, thudding down the narrow stairway, and even the Reverend Wada who hurried down the ladder from the church tower where he was hanging an enormous American flag.

"Mrs. Jamieson! Mimi! Mr. Nelson! Mrs. Nelson!" Yuki called out to each of them as they stepped out of the car carrying brooms and buckets and mops and rags.

"We came to help. Can you use some help?"

"We sure can!"

"Come in, come in."

There was such a commotion of greeting and hugging, with the Wada children screaming and running around everybody, that Yuki didn't even notice Mr. Oka hadn't come down. It was only when they all sat down to eat the fried chicken and potato salad Mrs. Nelson brought for lunch that he finally came downstairs, and only after he was called twice. Then he sat at the end of the table and hardly said a word to anyone.

Yuki saw Mrs. Jamieson try to have a conversation with him.

"Would you care for more chicken, Mr. Oka?" she asked. "Did you enjoy the potato salad?"

But Mr. Oka pretended he couldn't speak English, only nodding or shaking his head in answer to her questions, so he wouldn't have to talk to her.

After lunch when they all got to work and Mimi came upstairs to help Yuki finish cleaning her room, Mr. Oka vanished altogether.

Mimi stood in front of the mirror in Yuki's room running a comb through her long blond hair. She was looking at herself, but she spoke of Mr. Oka.

"That old man's a strange character," she remarked with a frown. "I don't think I like him much."

Yuki found herself defending him.

"He's okay when you get to know him," she said loyally. "He's just sort of different."

Mimi shrugged. "Oh well, I don't really care," she said, and taking one last look at herself, she asked, "Did I ever write you about the new boy in class? He's got the bluest eyes I've ever seen."

That night at supper Yuki asked Mr. Oka where he'd been all afternoon. Without waiting for an answer she asked, "Didn't you like my friends?"

Mr. Oka thought for a moment. "They were all right for white folks, I guess," he said lightly, and Yuki could tell he didn't care a lot about them.

"Mimi was my best friend at school," she explained. But even as she said so, she knew Mimi was different. There was a space between them now, and it was hard to say why. Yuki just knew it was Emi now who was her best friend.

"Well, you'll like Emi and her grandma," she promised. "And I know you'll like Mr. Toda."

"Will I?"

"Sure, you just wait and see if you don't. And I know for positive sure you'll like my brother Ken. He was wounded in France, but he's getting therapy for his leg in an army hospital in Washington now. He'll be home pretty soon too."

Then the gathering would be complete. They'd all be together in a nice house Papa would find for them, and the days of waiting and longing would be over.

"Hey, Uncle Oka," Yuki said, "maybe if I just will it to happen, they might all be back next week, even Ken. Wouldn't that be super colossal?"

Uncle Oka nodded. "It could happen."

Maybe it could. Maybe it really could. A surge of joy streaked through Yuki, making her want to shout at the whole world.

"Yahoooo!" she sang out, causing Hokusai to let out a terrible screech, leap from Uncle Oka's arms and escape down the dark hallway.

Suddenly the dingy room seemed too small to hold her bursting spirits. Yuki rushed downstairs and outside where the Wada children were whooping and hollering around a roaring trash fire.

"Hey, maybe they'll all be back next week," she shouted into their hot, glowing faces.

They didn't know what Yuki was talking about, but they jumped up and down and clapped their hands and danced around the blazing fire with her, as though she'd just told them the war had come to an end.

Chapter 9

"WE'RE coming! We're coming!" Emi wrote. She sent Yuki the time and date their train would arrive, and underlined everything three times. "See you SOON," she scribbled all around the border of the page.

There were cots in all the rooms of the old house behind the church now, and it was ready for the Japanese who were coming home from the camps. Students from the campus church had come with ladders and brushes and buckets of paint and made the walls the color of pale sunshine. They sang as they worked, making the house echo with friendly sounds, and when they'd finished, it was as though the old house had been roused from a long, dark sleep. Yuki hardly recognized her room with its fresh coat of paint and new curtains at the window, and now there were two cots beside her own, for Emi and her grandma.

"What time does their train come in?" Yuki asked Papa for the third time since lunch.

"It's still the same, Yuki, four twenty. They're an hour late."

In two hours and fifteen minutes and forty-five seconds they'd be here. Yuki ran upstairs and inspected everything once more. Mama had helped her put fresh linen and blankets on the two extra cots just that morning, and now Yuki brushed a hand over each of them, smoothing out every small wrinkle she saw. She admired again the big sign she'd made out of cardboard with the bright crayon lettering, "Welcome home, Emi and Grandma Kurihara." She added a few flowers and curlecues and stars around the sign for Mr. Toda and put it on his cot in the room he would share with Mr. Oka. Then she was ready. It was time to go to the station.

The last few minutes of waiting were always the hardest. Yuki looked down the tracks dozens of times while Papa talked to the man from the mortuary who would take Grandpa Kurihara's coffin from the train. Finally she saw the engine chuffing toward her, pulling the train over the same hundreds of miles she'd traveled herself, gliding over the rails that wound over deserts and plains like a pair of shiny snakes.

"Here it comes, Papa. Here it comes."

The train pulled into the station, hissing and grinding to a slow stop. Yuki ran along side, trying to find Emi among the blurred faces peering from inside.

"Papa, suppose they aren't on the train?" Yuki began. "Suppose the bus from Topaz didn't get to the station in time and they missed it? Suppose there was an awful dust storm just when they were leaving and . . ."

"Yuki, will you please stop." And then Papa said, "There they are!"

He was right. It was Emi wearing the red dress her grandma had made for her when they were in Camp Topaz. There was her short, plump grandma behind her, moving slowly and carefully. She was carrying so many bundles and packages, she could barely hold onto the handrail.

"Emi! Grandma Kurihara! Here we are. Over here . . . over here." Yuki darted in and out among the other waiting people, calling out as she ran.

It wasn't until she'd hugged them both that Yuki noticed how sad they looked.

"Where's Mr. Toda? Is he still on the train?"

Emi shook her head, but said nothing. Her grandmother bit her lip and looked at Papa with a sad, puzzled expression.

"Didn't you get the telegram from Topaz?" she asked.

"Yes, the one confirming your arrival time."

"No, no," Grandma Kurihara said, grasping Papa's arm now

to make sure he understood. "The second telegram."

It was Papa who was puzzled now. "A second telegram? Why, no."

Grandma Kurihara began to dab at her eyes with a rumpled handkerchief. "Then you don't know? How can I tell you? It was all so sad and sudden and terrible," she said, sobbing. "He was so looking forward to coming home."

Papa spoke gently to her. "Now, Mrs. Kurihara, please pull yourself together. What is it? Where is Mr. Toda? Has something happened to him?"

She nodded, sniffing. "We brought back two coffins on this train, instead of just one."

Yuki turned toward the baggage car and saw one pine coffin being lifted out and then another right behind it. One was Grandpa Kurihara's and the second had to be Mr. Toda's.

But how could Mr. Toda be dead? Just last week he had sent Mama his latest poem. "My leaping heart is home with you now . . . The frail body hastens to follow." Had his spirit come home then because it couldn't wait for his tired body? Had he known perhaps that he was going to die? Yuki shivered as though a cold wind had suddenly filtered through her soul.

Emi whispered to her. "They said he was too excited about coming back. He was standing in line for supper at the mess hall and he crumpled up like a heap of rags. His heart just stopped beating."

Yuki nodded. There was nothing she could say.

Mama wept when they told her, but she soon wiped her eyes and said, "We mustn't grieve too much. We should be happy that Grandpa Kurihara and Mr. Toda are together now, and they'll never be sad or lonely or afraid again."

Still Yuki didn't think it was fair. They had both wanted so badly to come home to California. Instead, they'd both died in the lonely desert concentration camp a long way from home. She ran upstairs to get the welcome sign she'd made for Mr. Toda. She tore it into small pieces and flung it into the trash can.

"It's not fair," she murmured.

Emi watched, her wide eyes dark and glistening. "People have to die," she said slowly. "And you have to let them go. That's what Grandma told me when my mama and papa died. She said the ones left behind have to be strong and keep on living."

Yuki was surprised how old and wise Emi sounded. Emi seemed to understand certain things far better than she ever could. Still, Yuki couldn't quite let Mr. Toda go. She had a lingering feeling of anger and loss because he had been taken from her so suddenly.

The next morning the Reverend Wada held a brief funeral service for the two men in the chapel. Mrs. Wada removed the covering from the reed organ and played "Nearer My God to Thee," and Papa said a few words in memory of the two men.

But Yuki wasn't listening. Instead, she remembered how Mr. Toda had been such an important part of her life ever since she could remember.

As Yuki listened to Papa's words drifting over her head, she sent one last message to Mr. Toda. "Be sure you link up with Mrs. Jamieson's captain out there, wherever you are," she said. "And look for Pepper too. Good-bye now, Mr. Toda. Good-bye forever."

By the time they got to the cemetery, a light rain had begun to fall. It shrouded the living as well as the dead, covering everything with hazy gray mist. Yuki held on to Emi's hand as they walked carefully over the wet grass, weaving in and out, so they wouldn't walk on the heads and stomachs of the people buried there. And when the graveside service was over, they all walked down the gentle slope of the road as Mama led them toward Hana's grave. She was the first one to notice and gave a small cry of anguish.

"What is it, Mama?"

"Hana Chan's flowering cherry tree. Look what someone's done to it!"

It had been chopped down and lay on the ground lifeless, its leaves withered and dead.

"Who could have done such a thing?" Grandma Kurihara wondered as she bent to touch the wounded place where the tree had been cut. "Someone who still hates us?"

No one answered her.

Papa picked up the dead tree and carried it to the trunk of the car. "We can put it up in the church yard and tie some bread on it for the birds," he said gently. "You'd like that wouldn't you, Mama?"

Mama could only nod. "That would be nice," she murmured after a few moments. "And we can plant another tree for Hana so it will bloom again next spring."

They went away quickly then, leaving the dead to rest peacefully in the quiet gray rain.

Yuki and Emi helped Papa plant the dead cherry tree and tie pieces of bread and suet on its branches for the birds. Yuki stepped back to admire the tree. It almost looked like a Christmas tree bearing gifts of bread for the birds.

Hana would like it, she thought. So would Mr. Toda. And for a moment it was almost as though they were both right there looking at the tree too.

Suddenly Yuki felt better. She no longer felt so bad about never seeing Mr. Toda again. It was all right, she told herself. He had come home after all.

Chapter 10

ON Monday Grandma Kurihara had a visitor. He was a tall, heavy man, pale and nervous, wearing a black suit that seemed too large for him. She called him *Sensei* and bowed many times before she hurried to make some persimmon-leaf tea for him.

"That's the priest from the Buddhist Temple," Emi whispered.

"Really?" Yuki was surprised. Somehow she expected a priest to be wearing a white robe and carrying prayer beads in his hands. "He looks just like anybody else," she observed.

"Sure, but he's special," Emi explained. "Grandma said so."

The news this special man brought, however, was not good at all.

"I'm afraid I have some very bad news," he said to Grandma Kurihara, spacing his words carefully because they were so hard for him to say. "Our temple was vandalized while we were away in camp, and the things you and the others stored in the basement . . . well . . . it was one of those unfortunate things. Someone broke in. The caretaker has fled. We have lost everything. It is all gone."

Grandma Kurihara's lips quivered. "Everything? My trunks with my valuables? My Satsuma plates and my husband's collection of sword guards? Our photograph albums and our good clothes?" She was naming her possessions one by one. "My refrigerator and stove too?"

The priest wiped his face with a large white handkerchief and his fingers moved nervously, as though seeking his prayer beads.

"I am so sorry," he said over and over, "but there is nothing to be done. I hear there are many others who lost what they thought was safely stored. Farmers have returned to find their orchards withered from lack of care. Nurserymen have come back to dead plants and shattered greenhouses. Promises have been broken and trusts betrayed."

Grandma rocked back and forth in her chair, sighing and

moaning. "But what am I to do? All my grandchild and I have left now are the four suitcases we carried with us into camp."

The priest tried to comfort her. "I promise to do whatever I can to help you," he assured her.

But when he left, Grandma Kurihara murmured, "What can one man do? What can anybody do?"

"We must all help each other now," Papa said, trying to make her feel better. But Papa was having his own troubles too.

"Nobody seems to want to hire an enemy alien on parole," he said gloomily. "And all the jobs and houses have been taken by defense workers who moved here while we were gone."

Mama tried to cheer him up. "The war will end soon, Papa," she consoled. "You said yourself Japan can't go on fighting much longer. And when the war ends, you won't be an enemy alien anymore."

Mama was right. The war did end soon after, when the United States dropped atomic bombs on Hiroshima and Nagasaki.

Yuki and Emi were listening to the radio when they heard the announcement that Japan had accepted the terms of the United States and had surrendered.

"Hey, Japan's surrendered! The war's over!"

They ran downstairs, shouting to anybody who was around to listen. They almost stumbled over Mr. Oka sitting on the front steps holding Hokusai in his lap.

"Uncle Oka, have you heard? The war's over!"

"Japan finally gave up," Emi said, bending over to speak into his good ear. "The war's over!"

"I know," Uncle Oka said without looking up. "I heard."

"Then why do you look so sad? Aren't you glad?"

Uncle Oka looked up at last. "How can I be glad when my brothers and their families were burned to death by that monstrous atomic bomb?"

Yuki gasped. "They lived in Hiroshima, Uncle Oka?"

The old man nodded. "There were beautiful green fields of rice around my father's house," he said, remembering a time long past. "When I was small I could hide in them for hours and no one could find me except the crows that wheeled around the sun in the bright summer sky."

It was as though all the years of Uncle Oka's life were coming together before his eyes, and in the same instant, he knew that everything was lost forever.

Yuki and Emi sat down beside him trying to share his grief, and the Japanese part of each of them understood his sadness.

Yuki reached for his cat and rubbed the silky softness of its throat until it began to purr. She hoped Uncle Oka understood that she was telling him she cared about him too.

"Ah well," he sighed at last. "In war nobody wins. Nobody at all."

When Mrs. Jamieson heard of the surrender, she went straight to her kitchen, put on her apron, and baked her best sour cream coffee cake. Then she called a taxi and told the driver to rush her to the Japanese church. When she arrived, she found Yuki and Emi still sitting with Mr. Oka on the steps of the house in back.

She looked at them, and for the first time in her life, she seemed to have run out of words. She dabbed at her eyes with a lacy blue handkerchief and then thrust the cake at Mr. Oka.

"What can I say?" she asked. "Whenever I have no words to say what is in my heart, I bake a cake and just hope it somehow carries all the thoughts I cannot seem to speak."

The old man nodded briefly, but no one knew whether he understood what he was trying to say.

Mrs. Jamieson thought how his heart must ache for his homeland and the family he'd lost. She imagined, too, that for Yuki's mother and father there was joy that peace had come to the two countries they loved. But through that happiness there probably ran a deep current of sadness for those they had left behind in Japan. She brushed her hands together now, as though disposing of her private thoughts. "Well, at last your mama and papa are no longer 'enemy aliens,' Yuki."

"Thank goodness," Yuki agreed. She'd always hated their being called enemies, as though the war had suddenly made them different people when they'd always been the same caring people who loved America just as they loved Japan.

Mrs. Jamieson shook a ringed finger at her. "And just you wait. One of these days our country will pass a law so they can become citizens too, just like anybody else. Imagine," she said to Mr. Oka, as though he weren't aware of it, "having a law that keeps all Asian people from becoming citizens. Such utter nonsense!"

She was getting stirred up now as she always did when she thought of life's injustices. And as though she couldn't waste another minute, she hurried inside to see Yuki's mother and father. After she'd talked to them, she spoke again to Yuki.

"I'm going right home and write to President Truman," she said with a determined look. "It's time we changed a lot of things in this country."

Then she rushed as fast as her lame leg would allow to the waiting taxi, and as quickly as she had come, Mrs. Jamieson was gone.

The end of the war brought many changes to life at the hostel, for now all the Japanese in the camps were being sent back to California. Each day more and more of them arrived, tired and worn, carrying bulging bundles and dusty suitcases, worried and anxious about beginning their lives over again. There were army cots everywhere now—in the halls and classrooms of the church and in every room of the house in back.

"Golly, I'm beginning to feel like I'm back in camp again," Emi complained, as she and Yuki stood waiting to get into the bathroom.

"Me too," Yuki sighed. "What'll we do if the people just keep on coming?"

"Escape someplace, I guess."

"But where?"

That was the problem. There was nowhere for them to go.

One morning Papa lingered at the breakfast table for a second cup of coffee and Mama came from the kitchen to join him.

"I think it's time for us to move out and make room for the newcomers from camp, Mama."

"I was thinking the same thing," she answered, nodding. "But where can we go?"

Papa beckoned to Mr. Oka and told Emi to go call her grandma. As soon as Grandma Kurihara arrived he said, "I've had this idea spinning around in my head for some time now. We all need work and a place to live. We each have some money but not enough to start alone. So it makes sense for us to pool our resources and go into business together, doesn't it?"

Uncle Oka poured three heaping spoonfuls of sugar into his coffee and stirred it slowly. "If I'm thinking what you're thinking, I say maybe you are a little bit crazy, but also very wonderful." He looked at Papa hopefully. "What kind of business were you thinking of?"

Papa grinned. "The same one you were, Mr. Oka."

Grandma Kurihara fidgeted nervously in her chair. "I wish you gentlemen would stop talking in riddles and tell this old lady what it is that's whirling around in your heads."

But Mama had guessed. "If I'm not mistaken, I think they're speaking of Mr. Oka's Sunshine Grocery. Am I right?"

"That's it exactly," Papa admitted. "Then Mr. Oka could have his old store back, and Mrs. Kurihara, you and your husband owned a grocery store before the war, didn't you? Well, we could make good use of your experience now. And my job would be to keep the books and do the paperwork."

"That'd be super," Yuki began. But Papa wasn't finished.

"If we can raise five thousand dollars in cash for the stock and the fixtures in the shop and take over the lease, the shop is ours. And the best part is," he added with a wide smile, "there's an apartment above the shop with three bedrooms."

Everybody began to talk at once. Uncle Oka and Papa began to scribble on some paper, figuring what each of them could contribute. But Grandma Kurihara suddenly rose and left the room.

"Grandma!" Emi called after her. "Where're you going? Don't you want to be part of the shop?"

Mama looked disappointed. "Maybe she needs a little time to think about it, Emi. After all, she's had her heart set on buying back her own shop in San Francisco for a long time."

"But it won't be any fun without Grandma Kurihara and Emi," Yuki said dismally. Why did Emi's grandma have to be so difficult?

But in a few minutes, the old woman came pattering down the stairs, almost losing the zoris on her feet in her rush. She sat down beside Papa and placed in front of him a small purple satin pouch, drawn together with a black silk cord.

"There," she said with a pleased look. "I had that hidden in the toe of my Sunday shoes."

Papa opened the pouch and counted the wad of neatly folded bills he found inside. It was not a very large amount, but he knew it was all the money Grandma Kurihara had in the world.

"Thank you very much, Mrs. Kurihara," he said with a bow. "Yours is the first contribution to our new business."

Mr. Oka drew in his breath and pounded on the table like an auctioneer. "Done!" he said. "We're in business. The Sakane-Oka-Kurihara partnership has begun."

And they all shook hands on it. Even Yuki and Emi.

"Now we can all live together above the shop," Yuki announced, sounding like Emi's grandma taking charge.

She heard Uncle Oka mutter, "Not me, I'm staying here." But she really didn't mind. Emi and Grandma Kurihara would be coming with them, and they were moving out of the hostel to something like a home, even if it was only an apartment above a grocery store.

Mama and Papa were talking eagerly with Mr. Oka and Emi's

grandma now. They were laughing together, and they sounded different because their voices held at last the bright sound of hope.

Chapter 11

YUKI and Emi stood in front of the store, their heads tipped back, squinting up at the big new sign Papa and Uncle Oka had put up. "People's Grocery," it read, and in the window there was a sign that said, "Everybody welcome."

"This is a lot nicer than Grandma's old store," Emi said, admiring the store's fresh coat of paint. It was the color of apples leaves, and she touched it now with the tip of her finger to see if it was dry.

"Uncle Oka says it looks ten times better than when he had it before the war." Yuki took a few steps back to get a better look and bumped into a tall man standing near the curb. He was in work clothes and carried a black lunch pail as though he were just going to work. Neither of them had noticed him as he stood there listening to them admire the shop.

"You people taking over?" he asked. His voice was flat and controlled. It had no hint of either friendliness or hate. He wasn't smiling, but he wasn't frowning either.

Yuki looked at his hard blue eyes. "My papa and his friends just bought it," she answered proudly. "It's going to be the best grocery store around here."

Yuki smiled at him and was immediately sorry, for the man didn't smile back. He closed himself off, making her feel small and worthless. She stopped talking, but now Emi spoke up.

"My grandma is going to help run it too."

The man simply listened and turned the same expressionless look toward Emi. He acted, in fact, as though Yuki and Emi weren't even there. He seemed to have important and private thoughts in his head that had nothing whatever to do with them.

"I see," he said at last, and then walked quickly away from them down the street.

Emi shrugged. "He's weird."

"He sure is. He gives me the creeps."

They turned back then to admiring the store and didn't give him another thought.

While Yuki's mother and father worked to get settled in the apartment upstairs, Grandma Kurihara and Uncle Oka ran the store downstairs. The two of them were like a dog and cat, watching each other warily, neither one quite certain what to make of the other.

Uncle Oka wasn't sure how to handle the talkative old woman who wanted to be in charge. "Doesn't she know that I, Kunisaburo Oka, ran this very store for fifteen years before the war?" he grumbled to Yuki. "Doesn't she know I don't need a bossy old woman to tell me how to run my business?"

And Grandma Kurihara on her part would complain to Emi about having the old man underfoot all the time. It was a good thing, she said, that he was staying at the hostel and not living with them in the apartment.

"Don't you like him, Grandma?" Emi asked.

"Well, I suppose he is clever about getting the best produce at the best prices," she admitted. "And he does work hard, going down to the wholesale market to buy it every morning at four o'clock."

That was about as close as she came to saying anything nice about him. Still, when she felt the need to go to the cemetery and talk to Grandpa Kurihara on a Sunday afternoon, it was usually Uncle Oka who took her there in the battered truck he'd bought. Grandma would murmur her *Namu Amida Butsu* beside Grandpa's grave. Then, sometimes, she would produce two cold sausages and some bread from her bulging handbag, and the two of them would sit in the truck and have a snack beside the slope of the grave-dotted grass.

Sometimes Mama worried that Mr. Oka and Grandma Kurihara weren't getting along in the shop. But Papa said they were doing fine, and he spent most of his time upstairs unpacking their belongings. All the things they'd packed in such a hurry now began coming out of storage and friends' basements and attics, like long-lost children coming home. Papa didn't think they should get everything at once, but Mama was anxious to live again with her own things. "I want to sit in my old rocker," she explained, "and use my sewing machine and have all my books around me again even if I don't have time to read them."

The apartment soon became an impossible jumble of furniture and cartons and packing boxes, and it almost seemed like those frantic days when the army had given them ten days to get out. But this time they were unpacking all the familiar objects of their past life. It was like being propelled backward through time, and Yuki felt as though she were seeing small pieces of her old self coming out of each carton.

"Hey, Emi, look. Here's my old Orphan Annie mug. And here're my old diaries and my box of beads, and wait a minute, I'm going to look for Mrs. Jamieson's pearl ring."

Yuki waded through the crumpled newspapers that came billowing out of the cartons and went to look inside Mama's big brown trunk that had been in storage. She knew exactly where to look, and she found the small black velvet box she'd hidden inside a pair of red socks. She lifted the gold ring from its white satin nest and held it out for Emi to see.

"Oooooh, it's beautiful. Why don't you wear it to church on Sunday?"

Yuki shook her head. "I'm saving it."

"What for? Your wedding day?"

"Not for *that* long. I told Mrs. Jamieson I'd wear it to celebrate when we were back home once more."

"Well, you're home now, aren't you?"

"Not really. I'm waiting till we move back to a real house."

"Oh."

Yuki didn't notice the disappointment in Emi's voice. She was rummaging about in another carton now and pulled out one of Ken's old records. "This was Ken's favorite," she said, and as she put the record on the player the slow sweet strains of Glenn Gray's orchestra filled the room. "I will gather stars out of the blue . . . for you . . . for you . . ."

Suddenly, Yuki had the most terrible longing to see Ken again. "I wonder when he's ever coming home?" she murmured.

"Probably not till the doctors are good and ready to let him go," Emi answered dismally.

Ken was still in the army hospital in Washington, but as far as Yuki was concerned, he might just as well have been in France.

"I guess you're right," she said with a sigh. "I guess he won't be home for a long time yet." And she put the record away carefully into its jacket and pushed it back into the carton of Ken's belongings.

For Yuki, one of the best things to come out of storage was her own bed and mattress with the curves and lumps in just the right places. It felt wonderful to curl up in it again, as though her body had found its old nest.

Papa put a rollaway bed in Yuki's room for Emi, and the two of them whispered and giggled and talked every night until Mama or Papa rapped on the walls and told them to go to sleep.

One night Emi whispered in the darkness. "Where will your brother sleep when he comes home?"

ELDEN D. FINLEY
JR. HIGH SCHOOL LIBRARY

Yuki guessed Emi was worried that she and her grandma would have to move out when Ken came home. She had worried about that herself, but now it seemed perfectly simple. "Ken can sleep on the sofa in the living room," she answered. "He won't mind. You'll see. You won't have to move out."

"Thank goodness." Emi sighed.

"Don't worry," Yuki whispered. "We'll take care of you forever." But Emi didn't hear her. She had already fallen asleep.

It was Grandma Kurihara's urgent shouting that woke them up with a start. It was only six o'clock, but she had already gone down to the shop. Almost immediately, she had rushed back upstairs, gasping and shouting.

"Fire! Help! Fire! Come quickly, Mr. Sakane."

Yuki tried to shake the sleep from her eyes, wondering if she were having another nightmare. But now she heard the sound of pounding feet as Papa rushed downstairs. And then Mama hurried into their room.

"Wake up, girls! Quickly! We've got to get out of the apartment. There's a fire downstairs. Hurry!"

This wasn't a nightmare. This was real. Already Yuki could see and smell the thin wisps of smoke that filtered upstairs. They rushed down into the shop where Papa and Grandma Kurihara were trying frantically to put out the smoldering fire. The shop soon filled with thick black smoke that stung at their eyes and made them cough.

"Yuki, run next door and call the fire department," Papa shouted.

"Hurry!" Mama called after her.

Yuki had never even noticed who lived next door in the old two-storied frame house. She ran there now with Emi close behind her. She pushed heavily on the doorbell while Emi pounded on the door.

"Help! Fire! Hurry!" they shouted together.

Finally a sleepy-looking man in a rumpled bathrobe came shuffling to the door. "What is it?" he asked.

"Fire!" Yuki shouted at him. "Call the fire department."

"Hurry!" Emi screamed. "Our store's on fire."

The man was wide awake now. He ran to the phone and in a few minutes they heard the shrill wail of the siren as the fire engine came tearing down the street.

Chapter 12

THEY all stood outside the shop watching helplessly as the black smoke billowed and writhed like an angry dragon and rushed out at them, making them cough and back away. Grandma Kurihara dabbed at her eyes with a big handkerchief, and Yuki wasn't sure if it was because of the smoke or because she was crying.

"They tried to destroy us," she said bitterly.

"Who, Mrs. Kurihara?" Papa asked urgently. "Did you see them?"

She shook her head. "I only heard the crash of the glass and smelled gasoline. Then when I saw the fire start I ran upstairs to call you."

The firemen put out the blaze quickly, pouring great streams of water on the shooting flames. They checked carefully to make sure the last spark was out, and they also checked the apartment upstairs.

The chief came to talk to Papa and listen to Grandma Kurihara's story. "I'm sorry it happened, Mr. Sakane," he said. "There are some who think they still have to fight the war against Japan right here. It's ridiculous, but it's happening." He wiped his face and pushed back his hat. "I'm just glad we caught it before you lost the whole building."

Papa thanked him and shook his hand. Then they all went in to see what was left of the store. The front window was shattered where a brick had been thrown. There was broken glass everywhere, and the whole store was flooded with water. Smoke had blackened the walls, most of the shelves were charred, and the counter was a black hulk of burned wood. Labels had been burned or washed off most of the canned goods and everything that wasn't in tins or bottles was useless.

"Oh Papa," Mama sighed. "Have we lost everything?"

Before Papa could answer, Mr. Oka came rumbling back from the wholesale market where he'd gone to get the day's produce. He rushed into the store shouting, "What's happened? What's happened? What's become of our store?" His eyes were glittering and his forehead was damp with sweat.

When Papa told him, Mr. Oka's shoulders sagged as though someone had put a bundle on his back that was too heavy for him to carry. He walked aimlessly around the store, kicking at the broken glass and the cans that had tumbled from the shelves. The veins at his temples were throbbing and his fists were clenched tight.

Suddenly he began to shout, "They aren't going to put me out of business again! They aren't! They aren't!"

Papa put a hand on his shoulder. "You're right, Mr. Oka. We're not going to let anybody force us to give up."

Yuki wondered why anyone would want to destroy their one small grocery store. What harm were they doing here? Who would do such a thing anyway?

And then Yuki looked up and saw again the man with the cold blue eyes who'd asked about their store. He peered briefly into the store, his eyes met Yuki's for only a moment, and then he walked quickly away.

Was he the one? Had he come back to see how much damage he'd done? Yuki felt a rush of anger boil up inside. But she also felt afraid, and she didn't like the sick feeling she had in the pit of her stomach. She hated it. Suddenly she found herself crying, and quickly she wiped away the tears with the back of her hand so no one would see her.

A small crowd of people gathered around the store now to see what the excitement was about. Mostly they were curious, but a few came inside to tell them they were sorry.

"It's a shame," one woman said, her voice touched with sympathy. "You'll open again, won't you?"

Then Yuki noticed the man from next door. She barely recognized him now that he was dressed in a plaid shirt and a pair of faded overalls. His sand-colored hair was thinning at the top, like Papa's, and his gray eyes were kind. He had an open face that seemed to reveal exactly what he was feeling.

He came straight to Yuki and asked if she was all right. He gave her a light pat on the shoulder to show that he cared. Then he turned to Papa. "Have you people had breakfast?" he asked. "My wife says for you all to come over and have some hot coffee and rolls."

"Ah, that's very kind of you." Mama and Papa murmured their thanks together.

"You must be cold," the man said.

It was only then that Yuki realized she was barefoot and shivering in her thin bathrobe. A thick gray summer fog still hung over the city and there was no sign yet of the sun breaking through. She looked at Emi and saw that she was shivering too. Her felt slippers were sopping wet, but she didn't even seem to notice. Like Yuki, she was numb. It was as though this whole thing had been a terrible nightmare.

"My name's Stephen Olssen," the neighbor said, as he led

them to his house. "We've been meaning to come say hello, and now this. . . . It's a shame."

When they were inside their neighbor's house, Yuki noticed something. "Where's Uncle Oka?" she asked.

"He wouldn't come," Papa said in a low voice. "He still has a lot of sorting out to do."

"In his shop?"

Papa shook his head. "No, I'm afraid it's inside his head."

Yuki wasn't sure what Papa meant, but now she couldn't worry any more about Uncle Oka, for Mrs. Olssen came out with a tray that held a pitcher of steaming hot chocolate, a pot of coffee and an enormous platter full of sweet rolls with butter melting over them in thick yellow swirls. Her long brown hair was swept up neatly into a large bun and she wore a blue apron over her skirt and blouse. There was something comfortable and relaxed about her manner that put them all at ease, and Yuki liked her immediately.

"My name's Emma," she began. "I meant to bring over some cookies when you moved in, but well, now you're all here. And I'm so very sorry about the fire."

Her words came out in a friendly stream as she poured cups of steaming coffee and mugs of hot chocolate.

"Now which of you is the older sister?" she asked Emi.

And quiet Emi suddenly began talking as though she'd known Emma Olssen all her life. She quickly told her that she and Yuki weren't sisters at all, and how they came to be living together. Then Mama talked, telling how she had a son who'd been wounded in the war.

"He must be about our Johnny's age," Emma Olssen said softly.

"Ah, you have a son in the army too?" Papa asked.

The smile faded quickly from Mrs. Olssen's face, and she looked to her husband to answer Papa's question.

"No . . . Johnny joined the marines," Stephen Olssen said briefly, and then quickly changing the subject he said, "Say, let me know when you need help repairing your store. I'm a carpenter by trade and I'd like to give you a hand with new shelving or whatever else you need in the store."

Yuki saw Stephen Olssen's strong arms and hands and felt his strength spilling out to each of them. Papa no longer looked so grim or tense, and Mama and Grandma Kurihara had begun to smile again. Yuki and Emi had both stopped shivering. Emma and Stephen Olssen had not only warmed them with their hot breakfast; their caring seemed to make the terrible thing that had happened a little easier to bear.

Emi's grandmother didn't say much at the Olssens; but when they came back to the store she said thoughtfully, "Well, we may still have a lot of enemies, but we know we have some fine friends too."

Yuki wished Uncle Oka would agree with her. She wanted to tell him about the good feeling she had about their neighbors. But Uncle Oka was busy sweeping out the water and the broken glass and the debris that was all that remained of their grocery store.

"You should have come next door with us," Yuki said eagerly. "The Olssens are really nice."

But the old man shrugged. "They are all the same," he muttered. And he didn't even look up from his work.

Chapter 13

YUKI stretched out on the sun-dried weeds she'd flattened with her stomach and looked around at the shimmering wheat-colored wall of weeds around her. She heard a slight rustle and the weed wall parted in front of her nose. Uncle Oka's cat stalked silently into her private space and brought her another of its gifts.

"Ugh, Hokusai! Did you bring me another mouse?"

But she reached out to stroke the cat's soft head and drew it close. "I know," she said, "it's a token of your friendship. Okay then, thanks a lot . . . I guess."

Having deposited the gift, the cat slipped away as quickly as it had come. Yuki edged back from the tiny gray corpse and allowed the weeds to hide it from view.

She lay very still then, listening, and wishing somehow that the little mouse would get up and scurry away. But the only sounds she heard were the sounds of the city.

She flopped over on her back and watched the clouds move across her part of the earth, as though someone were plucking wad after wad of white cotton and flinging them into a wide blue basket. Would they float all the way to Washington, she wondered, across the country and over the army hospital where Ken was getting therapy for his leg?

With Ken closer, it should have been easier to send him her mental messages, but strangely enough, it had become just about impossible. Yuki would close her eyes and try to picture Ken's face with the strong nose and the dark, thick-lashed eyes she coveted so greatly. She held him as close as she could in her mind, but he seemed almost farther away than when he was fighting in France. So now she wrote letters instead of sending messages.

She stuffed two pieces of chewing gum into her mouth, peeled off the letter she'd begun to Ken on her tablet and started over on a new page.

"Dear Ken:" she began.

"I really and truly do wish you would hurry up and come home. It's getting downright boring around here. Rev. Wada's over, but he's helping Mama and Papa. Emi and her grandma went off to visit friends in San Francisco, and here I am lying in the back yard with only a dead mouse for company!

"I'll even be glad when school starts. But I feel kind of scared and creepy about starting at a new school. Suppose nobody will talk to Emi or me? But then maybe that would happen even if I could go back to Jefferson now. Do you think so? I guess maybe Papa was right. He said nothing stays the same. Even Mimi's different."

Yuki shifted her wad of gum to the other cheek and thought about Mimi. Then decided instead to write Ken about their grocery store.

"It really looks neat now that Mr. Olssen helped us build new shelves and a counter," she wrote. "You'll like the Olssens. I like them almost as much as Mrs. Jamieson, and you know that's a lot. Hurry up and come home so you can meet them. And, Ken, write soon. Your ever loving and only sister, Yuki."

Yuki read the letter over and crossed out "write soon." "Answer immediately," she wrote instead. She knew very well, however, that Ken might not even answer her at all.

Ever since he had been sent to the hospital in Washington he hardly ever wrote home. And when he did, his letters just didn't sound like Ken. It was like the time in Topaz when he'd grown so strange and sullen and wouldn't eat with them at their mess hall. Mama had said then it was because he'd lost his freedom and needed to get back out into the world. Maybe what he needed now was to get out of the hospital and the army and come back home.

When he was home Yuki was sure he'd be once more her cheerful, good-looking, six-foot brother, the star forward of the Japanese Men's Club basketball team, who one day was going to become a great doctor.

She wouldn't even mind if he bossed her around a little or

ignored her and went off to dances and movies with his girl friends. He could do whatever he pleased, if only he'd just come home.

Mama worried about Ken too. Yuki could see it in her face whenever she read one of Ken's brief letters that only told them he was okay. But Papa reassured her. "He's all right, Mama. They're taking good care of him at the hospital."

And Mama would answer, "I know they're helping him with his leg. It's what's going on inside his head that I'm worried about."

And then one day the telephone rang and Yuki answered it.

"Hello?"

Silence.

"Who is it?"

Then a voice so low she could hardly hear. "Yuki?"

"Who *is* it?"

"Yuki, I'm back."

"Ken? Is it you, Ken? Ken?" Yuki was screaming now.

"Simmer down, Yuki. I'm at the station. I'll be home in a little while."

"Wait . . . I'll call Papa."

"No, don't call him. I'm getting a cab. I don't want anybody to come meet me. Just tell Mom and Pop I'm on my way."

"Ken!" Yuki shrieked, but he'd hung up.

"Mama! Papa! It's Ken. He's home. He's coming home!"

Mama began to cry and raced down to the shop with Yuki to tell Papa.

"If only he'd let us know. Why didn't he let us know he was coming?" Mama said over and over. "Why didn't he want us to meet him at the station? Papa, why are you just standing there? Do something!"

Papa was surprised speechless. "Are you sure it was really Ken?"

Yuki nodded. "I'm sure. I'm sure. He said he was at the station. He's back. He's really back."

Emi was just as excited as Yuki. The two of them squealed and hugged each other and didn't know what to do with themselves. It was as though someone had suddenly told them in July that it would be Christmas that afternoon.

Grandma Kurihara quickly took charge of things. "Well, if your Kenichi is really back, then we must have a celebration," she said scanning the grocery shelves. "Shall we make him some salad with a can of king crab? Or maybe we should open a can of nice tender abalone and slice it with cucumbers. Mr. Oka, do we have some young cucumbers? And maybe a good melon for dessert?"

Mama wondered if she had time to bake a cake before supper, but Mr. Oka was already squeezing his cantaloupes to find one that was just right and brimming with golden juice.

"We'll put a scoop of vanilla ice cream on top," he said. "A son returning from battle certainly deserves our best—especially one who volunteered from behind barbed wire."

"Ah, old man," Grandma Kurihara whispered hoarsely to him. "Must you spill out your bitter thoughts at such a time? This is a day for the Sakanes to be happy and proud."

The old man shrugged. "I know . . . I know . . . leave me be, old woman."

And then Yuki heard the taxi pull up in front of the store, and there was Ken in his uniform, with the 442nd insignia on his sleeve and the bright strip of campaign ribbons on his chest. He got out of the cab slowly, and then they all saw that he was using crutches.

Yuki knew that the shrapnel had shattered his leg. But she thought when he came home from the hospital, he would come home walking straight and tall, his leg healed and strong. It had never once occurred to her that he would come hobbling home on crutches. The pale, thin soldier she saw now didn't really seem to be her brother Ken.

Still, Yuki was the first to fling herself out the door and throw her arms around his neck.

"Ken!" she shouted, her heart about to burst. "You're home! You're really home!"

Ken hugged her back. "Some basketball player I'm gonna be, huh?" he asked softly.

Chapter 14

THERE were a million things Yuki wanted to ask Ken, and yet now that he was right there, sitting across the table from her, she couldn't seem to think of a single thing. Instead she just stared at him, knowing that something was different. There were creases fanning out from the corners of his eyes now, and he was so thin she could see his pale skin stretched taut over the bones of his cheeks and his jaw.

She saw him shift uncomfortably in his chair and use his

hands to move his right leg when it grew stiff.

"Does it hurt?" she asked at last.

"Not really," Ken answered.

Mama quickly changed the subject. She didn't want anyone to remind Ken of this terrible thing that had happened to him that might cripple him for the rest of his life. She was trying hard only to talk of pleasant things. With Papa helping, she told about the Henleys in Salt Lake City, and about how they had all bought the store together, and how good it was to have their belongings out of storage at last.

Ken listened, but he wasn't really listening. And he was so quiet, it was almost as though he were sitting there inside a glass cage. They could see him and he could see them, but somehow, they weren't connecting.

Yuki thought of the times when Ken had hardly ever stopped talking and would make her laugh until her sides ached. But Ken's bright, happy self had begun to drain away in camp, and now the fighting and killing in Europe had drained it away even more.

Mr. Oka was watching Ken closely. He stretched across the table and offered Ken a cigarette. Ken took it gratefully, let Mr. Oka light it for him and inhaled deeply.

"Maybe now you are sorry you volunteered?" Mr. Oka asked suddenly. It was as though he wanted Ken to spill out his pain and hurt right there in front of them for everyone to see.

Mama gasped and Grandma Kurihara glared at him, "Old man . . ." she began. But Ken didn't seem to mind his asking.

"I'm sorry, but not for the reason you think," he said quietly. "If I had it to do over again, I'd probably volunteer again. But the cost was too high."

Everyone thought Ken was talking about his leg.

"There'll be more therapy, won't there?" Papa asked.

"You'll be able to walk without crutches someday, won't you?" Yuki blurted out. She didn't see the pained look on Mama's face.

"Maybe," Ken answered slowly. "Maybe I will, and maybe I won't, but . . . well . . . it's only a leg."

Ken had lost more than the use of his leg in the bitter fighting, but he wasn't ready yet to tell them about it. What happened to him was still locked up inside.

Mama understood. "Ken, how about some hot coffee?" she asked, reaching for his cup. She knew Ken was in need of her comfort and her love, but she couldn't take this soldier, her only son, and hold him in her arms as she longed to do. So she offered only what she knew he could accept.

"Thanks, Mom. Some hot coffee would be good."

When Uncle Oka got up and began to look around for Hoku-sai, Yuki knew he was ready to go home to the hostel. He shook Ken's hand before he left.

"Rest well tonight, Kenichi." Then he let himself out into the night.

Grandma Kurihara wanted to give her room to Ken. "You should have a room to yourself," she insisted.

But Ken insisted just as stubbornly that he was sleeping on the sofa.

At last Grandma Kurihara gave in. "Very well then." She sighed. "But we'll have to talk about making some changes soon."

Yuki knew she was thinking about moving back to the hostel.

"You could move in with Emi and me," she suggested quickly.

"Sure," Emi agreed. "We did it before at the hostel. We don't mind your snoring, Grandma."

"Well, we'll have to see," the old woman answered, which at least meant she hadn't made up her mind yet.

Mama and Papa lingered in the living room to fix up the sofa for Ken, tucking in sheets and blankets, fluffing up pillows.

"You're sure you don't mind the sofa?" Mama asked. "We'll borrow a cot for you tomorrow."

"I don't mind, Mom. Honest."

"Well then, have a good rest, Ken. I can't tell you how good it is to have you home."

"I know. Thanks, Mom."

"You're sure you're all right, son? You'll be comfortable?"

"Sure, Pa. I'm fine."

"Good night then. Sleep well. It's good to have you back."

"Thanks. Good night, Pop."

Yuki waited until the night sounds of the apartment had died down. She heard Grandma Kurihara finish in the bathroom. She heard the sounds of Mama and Papa's talking voices grow softer and softer and finally stop altogether. She waited until Emi stopped asking questions about Ken and fell asleep. Then she crept out of bed and tiptoed into the living room.

She could hear the low, even hum of the refrigerator and the ticking of the wall clock as she passed the kitchen. She slipped noiselessly into the living room, tiptoeing as she used to do when she lived above the Henleys. She looked at the sofa and caught her breath. No one was there. The sheet had been thrown back and there was no sign of Ken.

The light from the street lamp filtered through the shade and

Yuki saw Ken sprawled in Papa's armchair, his bad leg thrust out awkwardly in front of him. He was smoking and staring off into space.

"Ken?"

"Hey, you still up, Yuki?"

"Uh-huh. I couldn't sleep."

"Neither could I. Too much excitement, I guess."

"You mean coming home and all?"

Ken didn't answer. He was deep in thought about times and places and happenings that Yuki would never understand or know about. He couldn't even begin to describe them or talk to her about them.

Yuki knew he was far away. She longed for him to get up and put his hand at the back of her neck and march her back to her room the way he used to do when she didn't want to go to bed. She wished he'd throw a pillow at her or poke her in the ribs or wrestle with her on the floor.

But Ken just sat there. She wanted to give him a hug, but there was something about him now that made her draw away.

"Ken?"

"Huh?"

"I'm glad you're back. I really am."

"Good. Thanks. You'd better go back to bed now, Yuki. It's late. Good night."

"G'night, Kenichi Sakane," she said softly, and hurried back to her room.

It wasn't until she was back under the covers that the flood of disappointment hit her. She suddenly realized that there was nothing more to wait and hope for. All these long months, she'd waited and longed for the day when Ken would come home so everything would be wonderful again, the way it was before the war. But now, here he was. Ken was back, and all she felt was empty.

Chapter 15

"HE'S gone!" Mama said, her voice quivering with alarm. "He isn't anywhere, and his bag is gone."

Ken had taken off without telling anyone, and no one knew where or why he'd gone. He had been home only for two days and on the third morning, he just disappeared.

Grandma Kurihara shook her head miserably. "Ah . . . ah, you see. It is all my fault. He needed a room of his own. I should have been the one to leave."

"No," Mama said firmly. "It is much more than that. It's something deep inside that's troubling him."

Papa agreed. "If only he could talk about it. If only he could let it out."

Uncle Oka was the only one who said he understood. "Suppose you'd gone off to fight for your country to prove your loyalty and to make it a better place for everyone. Suppose you'd done that and even lost the use of your leg doing it. And then you came home and found restaurants where they wouldn't serve you and barbers who wouldn't cut your hair and shops with 'No Japs' signs in the window. How would you feel? Wouldn't you feel everything you'd done was all for nothing, a total waste?"

No one could answer. Was that it? Was that what was bothering Ken?

At last Papa spoke. "Maybe that's so," he said slowly, "but I don't think that's the kind of ache Ken is feeling now. I think . . . well . . ." Papa's voice drifted off.

"Maybe he's worried about his leg," Yuki suggested.

Emi had another idea. "Maybe it got so bad he went to the Veteran's Hospital in Palo Alto."

"But he'd have told us if that's where he went."

It was a puzzle and no one had an answer. All they could do was wait.

At last Ken telephoned from Merced. He was at the home of his best friend, Jim Hirai.

"Thank goodness," Papa said, relieved. "You two must have a lot to talk about. Have a good time."

"No, Pa, you don't understand. I never wrote you about it, but Jim is dead. It's his family I came to talk to."

"Jim dead?" Papa couldn't believe it.

Jim was Ken's best friend. They had gone through high school together. They were both juniors at the University when the war broke out. They had worked together at the camp hospital in Topaz, and they had volunteered together when the army came to recruit for an all-Nisei combat unit.

Papa began to understand the shape of Ken's grief.

"I see," he said quietly. "Comfort them as best you can, Ken. And then come on home. We all miss you."

"Thanks, Pa."

"The trip was something Ken had to do," Papa explained. "Maybe now he'll be able to talk to us about it too."

"I hope so," Mama murmured, but she didn't sound very sure.

This time Grandma Kurihara made up her mind. "When Kenichi comes home, he is going to have a room of his own," she announced. "Either I move in with the girls or Emi and I go back to the hostel. Mr. Oka says there is room there now, and it would be simple to move back. After all, Emi and I have only four suitcases to our name."

"You can't go back to the hostel," Yuki insisted.

"And I won't go," Emi said, startling her grandmother.

Emi seemed a little surprised herself for speaking up to her grandmother like that. But after she'd done it once, she did it again. "I'm staying with Yuki," she said firmly.

And for the first time in many years, Grandma gave in to Emi. "Well then," she said amiably, "I guess I move in with you girls."

So now Grandma Kurihara's cot was squeezed in between Emi and Yuki's beds. The first night she moved in with them, she announced she had a bit of therapy she needed to do on her legs. "Standing all day in the shop doesn't help them one bit," she explained.

"You mean you've got some herb tea for tired legs?" Yuki asked.

"No, not that. Wait and watch. You'll see."

Yuki watched Grandma Kurihara sit on her cot with her legs stretched out in front of her. She had an old candy box beside her, and from it she took a slim stick of incense and lit it. She handed it to Emi. "Here, hold this for me," she instructed.

Next from a wad of the soft burning herb, *moxa,* she took a tiny pinch, smaller than a grain of rice, and licking it lightly so it would stick, she placed it carefully on the muscle of her leg.

"Now," she said to Emi.

Emi bent carefully over it and lit the tiny mound of *moxa* with the incense. The red heat flickered quickly through the *moxa* and burned down to Grandma's leg. The sweet smoky smell of incense and burning *moxa* drifted over them all, and the old woman sucked in her breath.

"*Ah ita, ah ita . . .*" She winced, rocking back and forth at the sharp pain. She sighed with relief when the *moxa* had burned out.

"Why do you do it if it hurts so much?" Yuki asked.

"That's what I say," Emi agreed. "You're crazy, Grandma."

But the old woman looked at them, surprised that they should be so stupid. "It hurts, but it's a good kind of hurt, don't you know. And afterwards, ah, there is such a feeling of relief."

She continued the process over and over again until she'd

burned six tiny pinches of *moxa* on each leg.

"It's a counterirritant," she explained. "The sharp pain of the heat makes the dull ache in my leg go away. Want to try? I'll show you."

"No-oo-oo," Yuki and Emi shrieked together.

"That'd be a thousand times worse than eating your essence of egg yolk."

"Or drinking your earthworm brew!"

Emi had already had enough of her grandma's doctoring, and Yuki knew better than to try anything the old woman offered.

That night Grandma Kurihara stayed up whispering and talking with them for a long while. Then she abruptly announced it was time for them to go to sleep. It was hard for Emi and Yuki to go on talking then, for she lay between them looking like a beached whale. When she told them to shush and go to sleep, that's what they had to do.

The night Ken came home from Merced, Grandma talked with them for a long time as they got ready for bed. "He's talking a little more now, did you notice?" she asked.

"But he's still not the same," Yuki observed. "He told Mama today he wasn't going back to college."

"Ever?"

"That's what he said. He said he didn't care whether he became a doctor or not."

"Well, I think he's nice anyway," Emi interrupted. "And he's handsome too."

"Of course he's nice and he's handsome." Grandma sniffed. "But Yuki is right. There is something still troubling him. If we could only find out what it is . . ." Her voice drifted off.

"Emi?" Yuki whispered over the hump that was Grandma.

"What?"

"You still awake?"

"Uh-huh."

"You know what I think? I think . . ."

Grandma Kurihara suddenly sat up in bed. "That's it! I've got it," she said. "What Kenichi needs is a counterirritant to get rid of the ache inside his soul. That's what he needs."

"Oh, Grandma, what're you talking about? Are you going to burn some *moxa* on Ken's soul?"

"Of course not, silly child."

"What then?"

"The old man," she said excitedly. "Mr. Oka will be our counterirritant. I'm going to have a talk with him tomorrow."

"What are you talking about, Grandma Kurihara?"

But the old woman sank down again in her cot and drew the covers up to her chin. She uttered a great long sigh and began to murmur her prayers. Long before she was finished both Emi and Yuki were sound asleep.

Chapter 16

KEN sat outside in back of the grocery store, letting the sun warm his body and comfort his leg. He leaned against the building, his eyes closed, and he tried to shut out the sounds that grated against every nerve. He couldn't stand the noise. He hated hearing the buses going by in front of the store, and he shouted at Yuki when she turned the radio up too loud. And when there were too many people talking in a room, he simply had to get up and leave.

He gritted his teeth now as he heard someone come out the back door. It was Mr. Oka, but he took care not to slam the door. He lowered himself to the ground beside Ken muttering something about his aching bones.

"I could use a little sunning too," he said quietly.

Ken nodded, his eyes still closed. But he couldn't ignore Hokusai who leaped lightly onto his lap.

"You know your sister threw a pillow at him the first time she saw him."

Ken smiled. "Sounds like Yuki. She never did like cats."

"How about you?"

"Oh I don't mind them. They're quiet. They come greet you occasionally, but then they go off and leave you alone."

The old man nodded. "Exactly right. That's exactly why I like having a cat for a pet. Hokusai's good company."

He offered Ken a cigarette and they sat smoking together. It was good. They weren't saying anything to each other, but the old man knew they were having a good kind of conversation anyway. They understood each other.

The next time the old man had a smoke with Ken out in the sun, he began another kind of conversation. He spoke carefully, knowing what he must do.

"You never should have gone, you know," he began.

"Where?"

"To join the army. Why did you have to be such a hero?"

Ken took a deep breath and looked hard at Mr. Oka. He knew this was a man who needed to hear the truth spoken clearly.

"I guess I went to prove we were just as good as anybody else . . . so kids like Yuki could come back to California and not be ashamed of being Japanese. And . . . well . . . I guess I believed in this country."

Ken felt foolish. He didn't like giving speeches even to one old man. He stopped talking.

Mr. Oka leaned closer to Ken and prodded further. "And did you accomplish all that? Did it do any good for you to go and get your leg blasted so you might spend the rest of your life being crippled? You know the world hasn't changed that much in spite of what you did. Isn't that what's churning at your insides now?"

Ken was silent for a moment. "Maybe that's part of it," he said grimly. "But that's not the worst of it. The worst is knowing that Jim's dead and I'm alive."

"But that's war, Kenichi. You were just lucky."

Ken sank back as though the breath had been knocked out of him. "It wasn't just luck. It was because Jim had to be a hero. He threw himself on a grenade to save the rest of us in the shell crater. I could have done it too, but I didn't. If I'd done it, I'd be the one buried over there in that foreign soil and Jim would be back here feeling the sun and smelling the grass."

Ken was crying now, without making a sound. "Damn, stupid, stinking war!"

Mr. Oka sighed. So that was it. Ken couldn't forgive himself because his best friend had died for him.

The old man knew what it was not to be able to forgive. The first week he was in America, lonely and friendless, he had been spat upon by a man in the street. And in all the years after, he had been denied the kind of life any man with white skin could have. So he had harbored a core of resentment that he had nurtured carefully through the years. And he told himself that one day when he had saved enough money, he would return to Japan where he would be as good as any other man walking the streets.

But the war had changed all his plans. He was still in America, beginning all over again, and he was too old and too tired now to go back to Japan. Why then was he still nurturing his hate?

He touched Ken's arm. "I understand your pain, Kenichi," he said.

He wanted to tell Ken it was time to forgive himself, but he didn't know how. So instead he went inside and told Ken's mother and father what they needed to know, so they could understand how it was with their son.

And when Papa heard, he knew what words he had to speak to Ken one day when the time was right and when Ken would listen.

When Grandma Kurihara heard, she brewed a pot of persimmon-leaf tea for Uncle Oka.

"Old man," she said with a slow smile, "you did your work well."

Chapter 17

THE short days slipped quickly now into long cold nights, and the maple leaves turned brown and fluttered to the ground with the chill winds that blew in from the bay.

Yuki and Emi had been going to Westview Junior High for almost two months now and nothing terrible had happened. Some people in class talked to them and some didn't, but Yuki could accept that because she knew that was just how things were going to be.

The worry about Ken continued like a dull ache for everybody. It was there and it didn't go away and no one could do anything about it. Ken didn't want to talk to anyone. And he wouldn't listen to anybody, not Mama or Papa or Uncle Oka or even the Reverend Wada who came many times to talk to him.

"Just leave me alone, will you please?" he'd say.

So they simply had to wait. But Yuki was used to waiting. She'd waited for so many things since the war, and now the end of the waiting seemed almost in sight. She hoped it would just be a short wait until Ken was his old self again, and Papa could find a real house for them that they could call home.

Ken, too, seemed to be waiting for something without knowing what that something was. He refused to go and register at the university. He hardly ever went out, and he didn't see any of his old friends who'd come back to Berkeley. Mostly he stayed at home, just sitting and waiting.

Now it was almost Thanksgiving, and there was a kind of stirring in Yuki's blood, a feeling of expectation that seemed stronger this year than ever before. This would be the first Thanksgiving since they were in camp that they could all be together as a family.

"We have so much to be thankful for," Mama said. "The war is over. We're back in California, and Kenichi is home."

She named her private blessings one by one, as though by saying them aloud they became more real to her.

"And we're invited to the Olssens for Thanksgiving dinner," Yuki reminded her.

That seemed like a very good blessing as far as Yuki was concerned. Mrs. Jamieson was invited too, and even Uncle Oka had agreed at last to go with them.

They trooped next door for Thanksgiving dinner looking like a small procession. Papa carried a pot of gold chrysanthemums, Mama took a pumpkin pie she'd baked, Grandma Kurihara took a jar of strawberry jam, and Mrs. Jamieson, looking glorious in an orange cape that almost matched her flaming hair, carried the biggest chocolate cake she'd ever baked. Uncle Oka took some cans of peaches and pears from the shop, and Yuki and Emi folded dozens of gold and red paper cranes to decorate the table.

"I guess I'm the only one to come empty handed," Ken apologized as he greeted Emma Olssen.

"But you brought yourself, Ken," she answered warmly, "and that means more to me today than anything else."

Yuki wondered why there were tears in her eyes when she spoke to Ken.

Ken walked over to the mantel and looked at the large silver frame containing the photograph of a young man.

"That's our Johnny," Stephen Olssen explained. "Just about your age, I imagine, Ken."

"Oh? Where is he now? Still in the service?"

Mr. Olssen glanced at his wife and Yuki saw her nod slightly. "It's all right, Stephen," she said softly. "You can tell them now."

"Our son was killed in Iwo Jima," he said in a voice so low Yuki could scarcely hear.

Mama gasped. "Your only son was killed by the Japanese?" It could have been the son of one of her friends in Japan who had thrown the grenade or pulled the trigger or thrust the bayonet that had killed Johnny Olssen.

"Oh, Mrs. Olssen, I am so very sorry," Mama murmured. She took Emma Olssen's hands in both of hers, trying to give something of herself to the mother who had lost her son.

Everyone tried to say something comforting. But Ken and Uncle Oka said nothing. It was as though they could find no words to say what they were feeling inside.

Yuki shivered as she felt the close sweep of death once more. And, suddenly, she was so glad Ken was alive and breathing and sitting right there that she got up, stepped carefully over his crutches and lame leg and squeezed herself into the armchair next to him.

"Move over, Ken," she said with a friendly shove. "I want to sit next to you."

"Sure," Ken answered. Yuki felt his arm slip lightly around her shoulder and she knew then that the glass cage was no longer there.

Yuki couldn't remember when she'd eaten such a wonderful dinner. The roast turkey that Emma Olssen carried in from the kitchen, plump and brown and glistening on its bed of parsley, was the biggest turkey she'd ever seen. And with it came candied sweet potatoes, string beans and carrots, and a beautiful cranberry salad molded into a fruit-filled star.

There was such a good feeling of closeness and sharing as they sat together around the big table that Yuki didn't want the day ever to end. She watched Uncle Oka especially. He drank glass after glass of the wine that Stephen Olssen poured for him. And soon, his face flushed and glistening, he began to talk. He told Mr. Olssen all about his life in America and of the terrible loneliness and anger that had filled it.

Stephen Olssen nodded and listened. "You've had cause for anger, Mr. Oka," he said at last. "But try now to forgive us if you can. Don't destroy yourself with any more bitterness."

The old man looked startled. "Forgive you?" he asked.

"Yes, all of us . . . if you can."

"Can you forgive the soldier who killed your only son?"

"I have already."

Mr. Oka shook his head. "Forgive . . ." he murmured. The word came slowly and softly from his lips, as though he were understanding it for the first time. He spoke the word as a blind man might feel a new object, touching it, discovering it, wondering about it, amazed at the feeling that came alive as he said the word.

Then he said slowly, "I guess forgiving does take the bundle of hate off your back. Still, when you've been wronged for so many years . . ." Mr. Oka paused. "Well, maybe there are ways to fight back without destroying yourself."

Then he glanced at Ken and a certain look passed between them. "I suppose we need to forgive ourselves, just as much as other people," he said.

But Ken said nothing.

No one had missed the words that Mr. Oka spoke, and Grandma Kurihara leaned toward him now saying, "Well, old man, maybe there is some hope for you after all."

Emi poked Yuki. "Did you hear?" That was the nicest thing she'd ever heard her grandma say to Mr. Oka.

But Yuki was watching Ken. She knew he was listening and thinking. What about Ken, she wondered. Was there hope for him too?

Chapter 18

LATE that night, after Uncle Oka had returned to the hostel and Grandma Kurihara and Emi had already gone to bed, Yuki sat with Mama and Papa and Ken in the living room. And she wouldn't go to bed because she couldn't bear to let go of the wonderful warm feeling she'd brought home from next door. If she went to sleep, it would drift away from her during the night and maybe never come back again. She wanted to hold onto the last of today just a little longer, just as she'd clung to Mrs. Jamieson and asked her not to go home.

But Mrs. Jamieson had put on her cape and hat and said firmly, "Yuki, my dear, you must let me go. Old Salt and Felicity and Marigold are at home waiting to be fed. Besides, you don't need me in order to hold onto your joy."

It was hard for Yuki to let go of the people she loved. She wanted them always to be near and close. She wanted them to close ranks around her, to keep her own small world safe and secure. She moved next to Ken on the sofa now, sitting as close as she could, feeling the fuzz of his sweater rub against her arm.

Mama's hands were folding some laundry, but she had a far off look, as though she were writing some poems in her head. Soon Yuki saw her put down the laundry and go pick up a notebook from the desk. She opened it and began to write, and Yuki saw that for once she wasn't scribbling on a margin or a scrap, she was writing on a fresh, clean piece of paper. It was as though she were finally freeing her poems from the fringes of her life and maybe freeing herself as well.

Papa was reading a newspaper, but Yuki saw him glance at Mama and see what she was doing. A smile of pleasure flickered across his face, but he was careful to hide it with his newspaper so Mama wouldn't stop what she was doing.

Ken sat silent, doing nothing, just staring and maybe thinking. Suddenly, as though he were answering a question someone had just asked, he said, "I might just go back East to finish college. Maybe I could even try for Harvard Medical School someday."

Mama and Papa quickly stopped what they were doing and exchanged a glance filled with their own private happiness.

It was Yuki who spoke first. "You mean you'd leave again?" she asked. "But you just came home. You just finally came back. Why can't you stay and go to school here?"

But Ken wasn't listening. It was almost as though he were straining to be free of the chair and his lame leg and this room and everything that held him here. And he was looking at Papa, not Yuki.

Papa had been waiting a long time to talk to Ken, and he knew now that Ken was ready at last to listen to the words he'd been wanting to say.

"Ken, you're a survivor, just as we all are—your mama, Mr. Oka, Grandma Kurihara and I. We're survivors from another land—the land of your samurai grandfathers. Their strength was our strength as we struggled to make new lives for ourselves in America. Make it your strength too, Ken. Hold on to it and be strong."

Papa stood up now and began to pace up and down. "Your friend lost his life, but you *have* life, Ken. You survived! Don't hate yourself for that. Just accept it. The way I see it, I think what you owe Jim Hirai and Johnny Olssen is life itself. You have an obligation to cherish this precious thing you have. Am I making sense?"

Papa stopped suddenly, as though he felt he'd said too much. "You'll make a fine doctor, Ken. I know you will."

Mama was nodding all the time Papa spoke, as though she were saying every word of it to Ken herself as well. She used the corner of a pillowcase on her lap to wipe her eyes.

"Oh, Kenichi," she said, "we'd be so proud of you."

Ken looked a little embarrassed. He pulled at his lame leg and looked at it a long time, as though he were studying every bone and muscle in it that he couldn't see.

"Well, I can still use my hands," he said slowly.

"Of course you can," Papa agreed. "And there's nothing wrong with your head, either."

"If he's got any brains left up there," Yuki heard herself say. And suddenly, she reached over and poked Ken in the ribs.

Ken turned and grinned at her. Then he reached out and gripped the back of her neck just the way he used to do.

"Okay, Yuki, that's enough out of you." He pushed her up off the sofa. "Get going, now. It's time you went to bed."

"Okay, okay, I'm going, I'm going."

And in that very instant, Yuki knew that the old Ken had come back at last. Everything had somehow fallen into place inside his head. And the curious thing was that almost at the same moment, everything inside her own head had come together too. She knew now that it was all right for Ken to want to leave. He needed to be free, and the reason he could free himself now was because he'd really come home at last.

Yuki went to her room and heard Grandma Kurihara and Emi making the soft, steady sounds of sleep. She looked at Emi and knew she was a survivor too. All she had in this world was this room and two suitcases and her grandma. But that was all she wanted. She wasn't waiting for anything.

And Yuki knew now that she was going to stop waiting, too. She groped her way to the bureau and opened the top drawer. Rummaging about, feeling with her fingers what she couldn't see, she found the small black velvet box with the ring Mrs. Jamieson had given her. She took it out and slipped it on her finger. Then she sat down on the edge of Emi's bed.

"Hey, Emi, look," she said.

"Huh? What? Is it time to get up?"

Yuki held out her hand so Emi could see the creamy white pearl that seemed to glow even in the darkness. "Look what I got out," she said. "I'm going to wear it to church Sunday."

Emi stretched, yawning. "Honest? How come? I thought you were saving it for when you could really celebrate moving into a house of your own."

Yuki shrugged. "I changed my mind," she said. "I'm not going to keep waiting any more. I decided I'm home right now."

Emi grinned. "Well, it's about time," she said. And she flopped over on her side and went back to sleep.

Yuki crept into her bed but she couldn't sleep. She looked around at the familiar dark shapes around her and felt safe and secure. She tried to think of some mental messages to send to somebody, but there were no more messages to send. Everyone she cared about was here with her now. They'd all come home at last, even Ken. And Yuki knew that everything was going to be all right. She'd finally come home too.

Connected
Readings

from
The Children of Topaz

Michael O. Tunnell and George W. Chilcoat

"TORA! *Tora! Tora!*" Shortly before 8:00 A.M. on December 7, 1941, these code words streaked across the airwaves from the dive-bomber of Commander Mitsuo Fuchida. They were a signal to the high command of the Japanese Imperial Navy that Japanese aircraft had just attacked the American naval base at Pearl Harbor, Hawaii. Up until then, Japan and the United States had not been at war, although World War II was raging on much of the planet. The Japanese air raid caught the U.S. Navy by surprise. On that sleepy Sunday morning, sailors and airmen could hardly man their battle stations before the Japanese dive-bombers destroyed or crippled almost all the ships and airplanes at Pearl Harbor and killed or wounded about 3,500 people. When the attack was over, a large part of the U.S. Naval Fleet in the Pacific Ocean was lost.

The United States immediately declared war on Japan. This was a nightmare for Americans, who had been hoping to stay out of World War II. And to make things worse, war with Japan automatically meant war with Hitler's Germany, because these two hostile nations, along with Italy, were allies. When Pearl Harbor was attacked, Germany already had been at war with the rest of Europe for more than two years. Now, American soldiers would be fighting and dying in both the South Pacific and Europe.

At home in the United States, people were angry and afraid. The war in Europe had seemed far away, and now it had come to America's doorstep. If the Japanese had attacked Americans in Hawaii, what would keep them from dive-bombing Los Angeles or Seattle? Fiery patriotic propaganda against Japan filled newspapers and radio broadcasts, and many Americans were overcome by an irrational hatred of anything Japanese—including fellow Americans who wore Japanese faces.

In 1941, there were about 125,000 people of Japanese ancestry, called Nikkei *(Neek-kay),* living in the United States, not including the territory of Hawaii. Most of them lived on the West Coast and, like the rest of the country's immigrant population, were usually hardworking, patriotic Americans. The problem was that because of their Japanese ancestry, they looked like the enemy. Of course, Germans and Italians were U.S. enemies, too, but German and Italian Americans resembled English and French Americans. Even though two-thirds of the Nikkei in the United States were born here and were American citizens, they suddenly became aliens and enemies in the eyes of many other Americans because of their distinctive skin color and features. One newspaper columnist even advised his readers to learn the differences among the Koreans, Chinese, and Japanese so that they could "be sure of nationality" before they were "rude to anybody."

People on the West Coast of the United States reacted violently to the Nikkei living there. But even well before Pearl Harbor, coastal residents resented them. In fact, the United States government always had denied citizenship to first-generation Japanese immigrants, called the Issei *(Ees-say)*. The Naturalization Act of 1790 limited the granting of U.S. citizenship to "free white person[s]," and although later amendments provided citizenship rights for Africans and even for other Asians, the Issei continued to be denied. In the Pacific states, they were not even allowed to own land or marry outside their race—in a country established by immigrants, no less! It was not uncommon to see billboards during the 1920s, 1930s, and early 1940s on the West Coast that read "Japs, don't let the sun shine on you here. Keep moving," or "Japs keep moving. This is a white man's neighborhood." Much of this racism was kindled when the Issei first arrived on the West Coast and, against all odds, became successful farmers. Because they were refused most other jobs and could not own their own land, the Issei took rocky, unwanted plots of rented land and converted them into thriving farms. By 1941, these farms were producing over one-third of the truck crops (vegetables) in California. Other farmers were jealous. Also, because the Issei were shunned by most Americans, they created their own society within a society in order to feel safe and to have friends. This made them seem even more remote and strange.

The children of the Issei, called the Nisei *(Nee-say)*, could not be denied U.S. citizenship because they were born on American soil. Unlike their parents, they tried to blend into American society as much as possible, sometimes even feeling ashamed of their "Japaneseness." Still, opportunities were not equal for the Nisei. One Nisei student recalled a high-school teacher discouraging him from selecting many of the majors that his white friends were pursuing in college. "Then the teacher told me out-

right in a very nice way that there was not much of a chance for
an Oriental to get a job in these fields. . . . I began to see that
they took us a little differently and we were not quite American
in their eyes in spite of things they taught us in the classes
about equality and so forth." Young Nisei engineering graduates
would end up as gardeners or store clerks because no one
would hire them. People joked that a creatively stacked fruit dis-
play meant the Japanese clerk was an engineer. Despite the fact
that Japanese-American students were consistently among the
highest achievers in school, discrimination persisted.

Therefore, when Pearl Harbor was attacked, people who already were prejudiced against the Japanese Americans suddenly had a reason to justify all their old hatreds. Restaurants
and stores refused service to the Nikkei. More nasty and threat-
ening signs appeared in shop windows and on billboards. Although the Nikkei as a group were extremely patriotic Americans, nothing they did seemed to convince other Americans of
their loyalty.

Japanese Americans were as stunned by the attack on Pearl
Harbor as the rest of the country. Many of the Nisei were furi-
ous. "*They* are attacking *us!*" yelled a Nisei high-school student. The Japanese American Citizen's League (JACL), an organization that battled discrimination by encouraging outspoken
patriotism among its members, immediately sent a telegram to
President Franklin Delano Roosevelt. It boldly stated: "We are
ready and prepared to expend every effort to repel this invasion
together with our fellow Americans." In days to come, the JACL
even organized war bond and Red Cross drives and worked
with the FBI to locate possible enemies within the Japanese-
American population.

The Issei were fearful and ashamed. Not only did they have
the faces of the enemy, but they were also still citizens of
Japan. Some of the elders tried desperately to cut ties with
their Japanese heritage by burying mementos such as samurai
swords and traditional Japanese clothing. They cleansed their
homes of Japanese language magazines and books, Buddhist
shrines (evidence of a religion strange to the Western world),
and even family photographs of relatives in Japan.

But neither the Nisei's patriotic words and actions nor the
Issei's efforts to appear more Americanized seemed to help. Destructive, unthinking reactions to Pearl Harbor erupted from the
worst personalities. In Washington, D.C., an unidentified "pa-
triot" chopped down several Japanese cherry trees in a senseless

act of anger. Japanese cemeteries were vandalized, as were the homes of Japanese Americans. Nikkei farms were terrorized, and, in a few cases, anti-Japanese fanatics shot and killed innocent people.

Even the more civilized elements of American society seemed infected by the war hysteria. Newspapers fanned the fire by continuing to print shocking and unfounded stories about Japanese Americans and using the same term for the Nikkei as was being used for the enemy—"Japs." Rumors about spies raced through communities like wildfire: the "Japs" in Hawaii had cut arrows into their crops that guided the attack force to Pearl Harbor; the "Japs" in California were in contact with Japanese submarines and were prepared to sabotage airports, power plants, or other military targets. Although some of these rumors are still believed today, there was never a single confirmed case of Japanese-American spying or sabotage. In fact, when President Franklin Roosevelt asked for a careful survey of Japanese Americans, it was reported that they possessed "a remarkable, even extraordinary degree of loyalty."

The U.S. government turned out to be as suspicious and mistrusting as any of the groups that were angrily pointing their fingers at the Nikkei. Within hours of the attack on Pearl Harbor, FBI agents broke into and searched the homes of respected members of the Japanese-American community—without search warrants. Then, over 1,300 men, mostly Issei, were arrested and taken from their families without any explanation. Yoshiko Uchida remembered the terrible worry: "All that day and for three days that followed, we had no knowledge of what had happened to my father." Probably for no other reason but their "Japaneseness," the arrested men were suspected of being disloyal. They were asked stupid questions, such as "If you had a gun in your hand, at whom would you shoot, the Americans or the Japanese?" (Most answered that they'd shoot "straight up.") In the end, 336, including Yoshiko's father, were sent to internment camps in Montana or South Dakota.

The Constitution of the United States guarantees the right to privacy, protecting people from having the police search their homes without authorization from the courts. It also guarantees the right to due process. "Due process" means that fair legal procedures must be followed before a person can be convicted of a crime. These basic rights, so fundamental to what the United States of America stands for, were simply cast aside for these Japanese-American men because they were deemed "enemy aliens." They were sent to internment camps without a fair trial, and, in the following weeks, nearly all of the Nikkei on the West Coast suffered a similar fate.

The people and the government seemed to demand that the Japanese Americans be treated as a threat to U.S. security. On February 19, 1942, President Roosevelt signed Executive Order 9066, giving the army the power to establish military zones in the United States "from which any or all persons may be excluded as deemed necessary." Although the order didn't specifically mention the Japanese Americans, the army immediately labeled the West Coast as such an area and then imposed an 8:00 P.M. curfew and a five-mile travel limit on all the Nikkei. The Japanese-American community was required to turn in any shortwave radios, cameras, binoculars, and guns—items handy to spies. Everyone knew that soon the Japanese Americans would be forced to leave their homes; the government would move them to special camps far from the coast. By the middle of March, the removal of "enemy aliens" began. Though the parents of baseball hero Joe DiMaggio were technically "enemy aliens"—they were Italian citizens living in San Francisco—no one dreamed of forcing them from their home. Yet the Nisei, who were United States citizens, were relocated.

Lieutenant General John L. DeWitt was in charge of moving people of Japanese ancestry away from strategic locations on the West Coast (airports, dams, power plants, the ocean front). He justified his actions by saying: "It makes no difference whether the Japanese is theoretically a citizen. He is still Japanese. Giving him a scrap of paper doesn't change him." DeWitt kept enlarging the areas from which he wanted enemy aliens removed until he achieved his goal: the relocation of virtually all the Nikkei living in California, Oregon, and Washington.

Comments by other well-known or powerful people only helped public opinion swing further against the Nikkei. Newspaper columnist Henry McLemore, who wrote for the influential Hearst publishing dynasty, was bold enough to say: "I am for immediate removal of every Japanese on the West Coast to a point deep in the interior. Herd 'em up, pack 'em off and give 'em the inside room in the badlands. Let 'em be pinched, hurt, hungry, and dead against it. . . . Personally, I hate the Japanese. And that goes for all of them." A farm leader in California openly admitted wanting to get rid of the Japanese for selfish reasons. "If all the Japs were removed tomorrow, we'd never miss them in two weeks, because the white farmers can take over and produce everything the Jap grows. And we don't want them back when the war ends either." It is not surprising that a Gallup opinion poll in early 1942 showed that while hatred for Germany was centered on evil leaders like Adolf Hitler, hatred for Japan was centered on an entire race of people.

Although the U.S. government permitted the Nikkei to voluntarily relocate to parts of the country farther inland, few had places to go or could afford to move so far away. Many of the five thousand who did move had a hard time. Some were met at the California-Nevada border by men with guns who turned them away. Even the governor of Kansas had the highway patrol keep Japanese-American travelers from entering his state.

Beginning February 25, 1942, the West Coast Nikkei began receiving orders from the U.S. Army to abandon their homes and move to the relocation camps. Usually they had to be ready to leave within ten days—ten days to store or sell their belongings, to sell or find someone to manage their businesses, to put all their affairs in order, and to pack only as much as they could carry. "How can we clear out in ten days a house we've lived in for fifteen years?" asked Iku Uchida, whose orders came on April 21. It was a question that was asked over and over by many families. Although the government stored the belongings of the Nikkei who had no other options, it was "at the sole risk of the owner." Many never saw their things again.

And who had to go? Anyone with a Japanese ancestor, even if the relationship was so remote that the individual had neither Japanese features nor ties to the Japanese community. And part-Japanese families—those with a white husband or wife— were not spared. Either they were separated or the white partner chose to go along with his or her spouse. Mary Kimura, a Portuguese immigrant, accompanied her half-Japanese son to the Topaz Relocation Center.

Nikkei families were registered and given a number. "From that day on," said Yoshiko Uchida, "we became Family Number 13453." Her family was given baggage and name tags with their number printed on them. They attached these labels to themselves and their possessions on E-Day (Evacuation Day). E-Day for the Uchidas, who lived in Berkeley, California, was May 1, 1942. They, like other families and single men and women, gathered at the First Congregational Church, toting as many of their belongings as they could carry. They were loaded into buses and taken to the Tanforan Assembly Center in San Bruno, California. Tanforan was one of several temporary camps where the Nikkei were held until the more permanent and remote relocation centers were constructed.

Taking only a few suitcases, the Japanese Americans left most of their lives behind—their friends, pets, and dreams for the future. One young Nisei put it this way: "You never thought such a thing could happen to you, but it has. And you feel all tangled up inside because you do not quite see the logic of having to surrender freedom in a country that you sincerely feel is fighting for freedom."

from
Farewell to Manzanar

Jeanne Wakatsuki Houston
and James D. Houston

ON that first weekend in December there must have been twenty or twenty-five boats getting ready to leave. I had just turned seven. I remember it was Sunday because I was out of school, which meant I could go down to the wharf and watch. In those days—1941—there was no smog around Long Beach. The water was clean, the sky a sharp Sunday blue, with all the engines of that white sardine fleet puttering up into it, and a lot of yelling, especially around Papa's boat. Papa loved to give orders. He had attended military school in Japan until the age of seventeen, and part of him never got over that. My oldest brothers, Bill and Woody, were his crew. They would have to check the nets again, and check the fuel tanks again, and run back to the grocery store for some more cigarettes, and then somehow everything had been done, and they were easing away from the wharf, joining the line of boats heading out past the lighthouse, into the harbor.

Papa's boat was called *The Nereid*—long, white, low-slung, with a foredeck wheel cabin. He had another smaller boat, called *The Waka* (a short version of our name), which he kept in Santa Monica, where we lived. But *The Nereid* was his pride. It was worth about $25,000 before the war, and the way he stood in the cabin steering toward open water you would think the whole fleet was under his command. Papa had a mustache then. He wore knee-high rubber boots, a rust-colored turtleneck Mama had knitted him, and a black skipper's hat. He liked to hear himself called "Skipper."

Through one of the big canneries he had made a deal to pay for *The Nereid* with percentages of each catch, and he was anxious to get it paid off. He didn't much like working for someone else if he could help it. A lot of fishermen around San Pedro Harbor had similar contracts with the canneries. In typical Japanese fashion, they all wanted to be independent commercial fishermen, yet they almost always fished together. They would take off from Terminal Island, help each other find the schools of sardine, share nets and radio equipment—competing and cooperating at the same time.

You never knew how long they'd be gone, a couple of days, sometimes a week, sometimes a month, depending on the fish. From the wharf we waved good-bye—my mother, Bill's wife, Woody's wife Chizu, and me. We yelled at them to have a good trip, and after they were out of earshot and the sea had swallowed their engine noises, we kept waving. Then we just stood there with the other women, watching. It was a kind of duty, perhaps a way of adding a little good luck to the voyage, or warding off the bad. It was also marvelously warm, almost summery, the way December days can be sometimes in southern California. When the boats came back, the women who lived on Terminal Island would be rushing to the canneries. But for the moment there wasn't much else to do. We watched until the boats became a row of tiny white gulls on the horizon. Our vigil would end when they slipped over the edge and disappeared. You had to squint against the glare to keep them sighted, and with every blink you expected the last white speck to be gone.

But this time they didn't disappear. They kept floating out there, suspended, as if the horizon had finally become what it always seemed to be from shore: the sea's limit, beyond which no man could sail. They floated awhile, then they began to grow, tiny gulls becoming boats again, a white armada cruising toward us.

"They're coming back," my mother said.

"Why would they be coming back?" Chizu said.

"Something with the engine."

"Maybe somebody got hurt."

"But they wouldn't *all* come back," Mama said, bewildered.

Another woman said, "Maybe there's a storm coming."

They all glanced at the sky, scanning the unmarred horizon. Mama shook her head. There was no explanation. No one had ever seen anything like this before. We watched and waited, and when the boats were still about half a mile off the lighthouse, a fellow from the cannery came running down to the wharf shouting that the Japanese had just bombed Pearl Harbor.

Chizu said to Mama, "What does he mean? What is Pearl Harbor?"

Mama yelled at him, "What is Pearl Harbor?"

But he was running along the docks, like Paul Revere, bringing the news, and didn't have time to explain.

That night Papa burned the flag he had brought with him

from Hiroshima thirty-five years earlier. It was such a beautiful piece of material, I couldn't believe he was doing that. He burned a lot of papers too, documents, anything that might suggest he still had some connection with Japan. These precautions didn't do him much good. He was not only an alien; he held a commercial fishing license, and in the early days of the war the FBI was picking up all such men, for fear they were somehow making contact with enemy ships off the coast. Papa himself knew it would only be a matter of time.

They got him two weeks later, when we were staying overnight at Woody's place, on Terminal Island. Five hundred Japanese families lived there then, and FBI deputies had been questioning everyone, ransacking houses for anything that could conceivably be used for signaling planes or ships or that indicated loyalty to the Emperor. Most of the houses had radios with a short-wave band and a high aerial on the roof so that wives could make contact with the fishing boats during these long cruises. To the FBI every radio owner was a potential saboteur. The confiscators were often deputies sworn in hastily during the turbulent days right after Pearl Harbor, and these men seemed to be acting out the general panic, seeing sinister possibilities in the most ordinary household items: flashlights, kitchen knives, cameras, lanterns, toy swords.

If Papa were trying to avoid arrest, he wouldn't have gone near that island. But I think he knew it was futile to hide out or resist. The next morning two FBI men in fedora hats and trench coats—like out of a thirties movie—knocked on Woody's door, and when they left, Papa was between them. He didn't struggle. There was no point to it. He had become a man without a country. The land of his birth was at war with America; yet after thirty-five years here he was still prevented by law from becoming an American citizen. He was suddenly a man with no rights who looked exactly like the enemy.

About all he had left at this point was his tremendous dignity. He was tall for a Japanese man, nearly six feet, lean and hard and healthy-skinned from the sea. He was over fifty. Ten children and a lot of hard luck had worn him down, had worn away most of the arrogance he came to this country with. But he still had dignity, and he would not let those deputies push him out the door. He led them.

Mama knew they were taking all the alien men first to an interrogation center right there on the island. Some were simply being questioned and released. In the beginning she wasn't too worried; at least she wouldn't let herself be. But it grew dark and he wasn't back. Another day went by and we still had heard nothing. Then word came that he had been taken into custody and shipped out. Where to, or for how long? No one knew. All my brothers' attempts to find out were fruitless.

What had they charged him with? We didn't know that either, until an article appeared the next day in the Santa Monica paper, saying he had been arrested for delivering oil to Japanese submarines offshore.

My mother began to weep. It seems now that she wept for days. She was a small, plump woman who laughed easily and cried easily, but I had never seen her cry like this. I couldn't understand it. I remember clinging to her legs, wondering why everyone was crying. This was the beginning of a terrible, frantic time for all my family. But I myself didn't cry about Papa, or have any inkling of what was wrenching Mama's heart, until the next time I saw him, almost a year later.

Baseball Saved Us

Ken Mochizuki

ONE day, my dad looked out at the endless desert and decided then and there to build a baseball field.

He said people needed something to do in Camp. We weren't in a camp that was fun, like summer camp. Ours was in the middle of nowhere, and we were behind a barbed-wire fence. Soldiers with guns made sure we stayed there, and the man in the tower saw everything we did, no matter where we were.

As Dad began walking over the dry, cracked dirt, I asked him again why we were here.

"Because," he said, "America is at war with Japan, and the government thinks that Japanese Americans can't be trusted. But it's wrong that we're in here. We're Americans too!" Then he made a mark in the dirt and mumbled something about where the infield bases should be.

Back in school, before Camp, I was shorter and smaller than the rest of the kids. I was always the last to be picked for any team when we played games. Then, a few months ago, it got even worse. The kids started to call me names and nobody talked to me, even though I didn't do anything bad. At the same time the radio kept talking about someplace far away called Pearl Harbor.

One day Mom and Dad came to get me out of school. Mom cried a lot because we had to move out of our house real fast, throwing away a lot of our stuff. A bus took us to a place where we had to live in horse stalls. We stayed there for a while until we came here.

This Camp wasn't anything like home. It was so hot in the daytime and so cold at night. Dust storms came and got sand in everything, and nobody could see a thing. We sometimes got caught outside, standing in line to eat or go to the bathroom. We had to use the bathroom with everybody else, instead of one at a time like at home.

We had to eat with everybody else, too, but my big brother Teddy ate with his own friends. We lived with a lot of people in what were called barracks. The place was small and had no walls. Babies cried at night and kept us up.

Back home, the older people were always busy working. But now, all they did was stand or sit around. Once Dad asked Teddy to get him a cup of water.

"Get it yourself," Teddy said.

"What did you say?" Dad snapped back.

The older men stood up and pointed at Teddy. "How dare you talk to your father like that!" one of them shouted.

Teddy got up, kicked the crate he was sitting on, and walked away. I had never heard Teddy talk to Dad that way before.

That's when Dad knew we needed baseball. We got shovels and started digging up the sagebrush in a big empty space near our barracks. The man in the tower watched us the whole time. Pretty soon, other grown-ups and their kids started to help.

We didn't have anything we needed for baseball, but the grown-ups were pretty smart. They funneled water from irrigation ditches to flood what would become our baseball field. The water packed down the dust and made it hard. There weren't any trees, but they found wood to build the bleachers. Bats, balls and gloves arrived in cloth sacks from friends back home. My mom and other moms took the covers off mattresses and used them to make uniforms. They looked almost like the real thing.

I tried to play, but I wasn't that good. Dad said I just had to try harder. But I did know that playing baseball here was a little easier than back home. Most of the time, the kids were the same size as me.

All the time I practiced, the man in the tower watched. He probably saw the other kids giving me a bad time and thought that I was no good. So I tried to be better because he was looking.

Soon, there were baseball games all the time. Grown-ups played and us kids did, too. I played second base because my team said that was the easiest. Whenever I was at bat, the infield of the other team started joking around and moved in real close. The catcher behind me and the crowd for the other team would say, "Easy out." I usually grounded out. Sometimes I got a single.

Then came one of our last games of the year to decide on the championship. It was the bottom of the ninth inning and the other team was winning, 3 to 2. One of our guys was on second and there were two outs.

Two pitches, and I swung both times and missed. I could tell that our guy on second was begging me to at least get a base hit so somebody better could come up to bat. The crowd was getting loud. "You can do it!" "Strike out!" "No hitter, no hitter!"

I glanced at the guardhouse behind the left field foul line and saw the man in the tower, leaning on the rail with the blinding sun glinting off his sunglasses. He was always watching, always staring. It suddenly made me mad.

I gripped the bat harder and took a couple of practice swings. I was gonna hit the ball past the guardhouse even if it killed me. Everyone got quiet and the pitcher threw.

I stepped into my swing and pulled the bat around hard. I'd never heard a crack like that before. The ball went even farther than I expected.

Against the hot desert sun, I could see the ball high in the air as I ran to first base. The ball went over the head of the left fielder.

I dashed around the bases, knowing for sure that I would get tagged out. But I didn't care, running as fast as I could to home plate. I didn't even realize that I had crossed it.

Before I knew it, I was up in the air on the shoulders of my teammates. I looked up at the tower and the man, with a grin on his face, gave me the thumbs-up sign.

But it wasn't as if everything were fixed. Things were bad again when we got home from Camp after the war. Nobody talked to us on the street, and nobody talked to me at school, either. Most of my friends from Camp didn't come back here. I had to eat lunch by myself.

Then baseball season came. I was the smallest guy again, but playing baseball in Camp had made me a lot better. The other guys saw that I was a pretty good player. They started calling me "Shorty," but they smiled when they said it.

By the time the first game came around, I felt almost like a part of the team. Everyone was laughing and horsing around on the bus. But as soon as we got out there, it hit me: nobody on my team or the other team, or even anybody in the crowd looked like me.

When we walked out onto the field, my hands were shaking. It felt like all these mean eyes were staring at me, wanting me to make mistakes. I dropped the ball that was thrown to me, and I heard people in the crowd yelling "Jap." I hadn't heard that word since before I went to Camp—it meant that they hated me.

My team came up to bat and I was up next. I looked down. I thought maybe I should pretend to be sick so I wouldn't have to finish the game. But I knew that would make things even worse, because I would get picked on at school for being a chicken. And they would use the bad word, too.

Then it was my turn at bat. The crowd was screaming. "The Jap's no good!" "Easy out!" I heard laughing. I swung twice and missed. The crowd roared each time I missed, drowning out my teammates, who were saying, "C'mon, Shorty, you can do it!" I stepped back to catch my breath.

When I stepped back up to the plate, I looked at the pitcher. The sun glinted off his glasses as he stood on the mound, like the guard in the tower. We stared at each other. Then I blocked out the noise around me and got set. The pitcher wound up and threw.

I swung and felt that solid whack again. And I could see that little ball in the air against the blue sky and puffy white clouds. It looked like it was going over the fence.

Can't Tell

Nellie Wong

When World War II was declared
on the morning radio,
we glued our ears, widened our eyes.
Our bodies shivered.

A voice said
Japan was the enemy,
Pearl Harbor a shambles
and in our grocery store
in Berkeley, we were suspended

next to the meat market
where voices hummed,
valises, pots and pans packed,
no more hot dogs, baloney,
pork kidneys.

We children huddled on wooden planks
and my parents whispered:
We are Chinese, we are Chinese.
Safety pins anchored,
our loins ached.

Shortly our Japanese neighbors vanished
and my parents continued to whisper:
We are Chinese, we are Chinese.

We wore black arm bands,
put up a sign
in bold letters.

No More War Games

James Leamon Forbis

When the Japanese attacked Pearl Harbor on December 7, 1941, James Leamon Forbis was serving as a coxswain on the USS Arizona. Here he gives a firsthand account of what it was like to live through this deadly surprise attack.

ON the morning of December 7, 1941, I was aboard the battleship *Arizona*. I was a coxswain. That morning I was in the duty section on the bow of the ship doing the morning chores. I had breakfast, and after cleaning up one of my jobs was to go back and rig the stern of the ship on the port side so the chaplain could have church services. I had a detail of six or eight seamen. There was an awning over the stern. This was the officers' country. We rigged great flags around, the international alphabet flags which were used for visual communication and which we also used for the services. We set up the portable organ, the pulpit and chairs. About the time we finished the bugler went on the fantail for morning colors. On normal Sundays they didn't use the band. The bugler took care of this function himself.

He had already sounded first call, which was scheduled for five minutes to eight. He was standing there awaiting eight o'clock when some planes came out of the east from Aiea. They were coming right out of the early morning sun and it was real bright. One of the seamen in my detail looked up into that sun. He couldn't see anything but he said, "Boy, I wish I was up there in one of them planes flying around this morning." I glanced up but couldn't see anything because of the blinding sun, and I said, "Yeah, I guess it's pretty nice up there." Then other planes started coming in over Hickam Field and the naval shipyard. They were dropping bombs as they came. Then they veered very sharply to the left.

Now, we were expecting the big carrier *Enterprise* to come in the day before and she hadn't come, so we thought, Maybe those are *Enterprise* planes. They were always playing war games out there, the army against the navy, in surprise attacks. So we thought, Maybe it's the crazy army air forces. They don't know when to quit. They even have to get after us on a Sunday morning.

When we had been out to sea previous to this, these army air corps pilots would come around and make runs on us and then drop little smoke bombs off the bow or the stern or the port so many yards out. They probably had sandbags with flares that'd make smoke. So this day we thought, That is what they are going to do.

But then the bombs were dropping and you could hear them exploding and *bang!*—one of them hit the bow of the ship. I told somebody with me, "Boy, somebody's going to get it now. They hit the ship." I still thought it was practice, but it was awful heavy for practice because it jarred that battleship.

Now we had been trained to close all the watertight doors and hatches in our part of the ship when air attacks started, so right away we did that. Then we were supposed to fill in on the anti-aircraft battery. We ran up on the boat deck where the antiaircraft battery was, but it was already fully manned and firing.

Very shortly we knew they were Japanese planes. There was nothing for us to do but stand around, and that wasn't very safe because we were getting some shrapnel and strafing. Now our battle stations were in number-four gun turret, which was on the after part of the ship. So we went down to the third deck and aft to the powder-handling room and then started climbing up the ladder to the gun turret, for our station was up in the turret. I was on the ladder when a bomb hit on top of the turret. It ricocheted off and knocked me down to the lower handling room. There was a kind of flash and we got smoked out. You couldn't breathe that old stink in there, that smell. I got burned, but not bad. We all got scorched. Then we went over into number-three lower handling room. The compressed air lines had broken there and the compressed air was blowing the smoke out so you could breathe and live.

The last word that came over the public-address system was, "Fire on the quarterdeck." Well, number-three turret barbette sat on the quarterdeck area, and part of the gun-turret crew was there in the turret. One of the turret officers was in the turret and he was keeping us informed. He says, "There's nothing that we can do." We couldn't fire the main battery at the planes, for the guns were fourteen-inch, not lightweight antiaircraft weapons.

Another man and myself tried to get down to the after steering room of the ship, for we knew there were some gas masks stored there. We got down there in the dark—I don't know how we did, except that we knew that part of the ship pretty well. Well, we got down there, but the masks were locked up and we couldn't get to them, so we came back to number-three turret. There the officer was holding all of the number-three and number-four turret crew, at least half of the full crew. We stayed up in the pits. The bloomers were off the guns so the smoke was coming in around them. Evidently oil was burning. The uniform of the day at that time was white shorts and skivvy shirts. The only way we could think about keeping that smoke out was to take our undershirts off and our white shorts and cram them around the guns.

We stayed there until the officer told us to come out. We went down the ladder to the main deck, which was burning just a short distance above the break where the boat deck starts. From there the wind and the tide were coming out of the east and keeping the oil and the fire back from number-three and number-four turrets. I had my shoes off. I don't know why. They were shined shoes and I didn't want to wade in that water and oil in clean shined shoes. I don't know what I was thinking. I wasn't thinking.

When I came down that ladder with those shoes in my left hand I stepped in oil and water up to my knees. The stern part of the ship was sticking up dry. The ship was down by the bow and sitting on the bottom. I walked around number-four turret. It was dry. I set my shoes down under the overhang with the heels against the barbette, just like I was going to come back and get them.

Everything was really in a sad shape. It was torn up. There was bombing, burning, and people were in the water. Some boats were retrieving them. Lieutenant Commander Samuel Fuqua was on the stern. He was directing some operations— boats to pick up men and things of that sort. Everyone was leaving the ship. There were about a half-dozen of us getting some life rafts over the side to the men in the water. Some of them had been blown into the water and some of them had jumped.

About the time we came out of the pits the USS *Vestal* was tied alongside trying to get under way. Her mooring lines were over our heads. Turkey Graham, one of the *Arizona* men, had a fire axe and he was chopping the lines. I can recall somebody hollering and saying, "Hey, don't cut our mooring lines, we might need them." But Turkey went ahead and swung that axe and told them, "Get out of here while you can." I understand that later he got the Navy Cross for that. We got some rafts into the water but the wind and the current were so strong they would carry the rafts right up to the fire. Meanwhile the boats were

picking men off the rafts, and this at least gave them a temporary refuge and a little relief from the oil. It was really thick.

A few of us remained on board ship. We had briefly discussed
the powder magazines. The fourteen-inch powder was directly
below us. Once in a while somebody would say something about
it. We knew the magazines were overdue. They were going to go.
And we knew that if they did go, that deck would blow us awful
high. So we got all the rafts over, and because there was nothing left for us to do we jumped into the water.

The old boat boom on the starboard side had been blown or
knocked loose from its anchoring. It was still attached but it
was in the water under the oil and you couldn't see it. I jumped
in and hit it. I was almost knocked out, just about unconscious.
One of the guys helped me recover and encouraged me until I finally could swim on my own. I started out half cuckoo from hit-
ting that boat boom. He stayed with me. We swam over to the
boat landing through the oil. I don't know how I made it. The
good Lord was looking out for us.

I was really pooped when I got over there, swimming against
the wind and the current and in that oil. I tried to climb up over
the side of the launch when both I and it were covered with
grease. It was quite a chore. I hollered up, and it so happened a
friend of mine saw and heard me. I just can't imagine how he recognized me because I was greasy from one end to the other. He
reached down and tried to hold on to me, but his hands slipped
right off. So finally he turned around and hollered for help. "Some
of you guys help me, here's Forbis down in the water." They
pulled me up. I was more dead than alive. But it was only a temporary thing. I wasn't burned and had no serious injury.

When I got in that boat and looked back I got the full impact
of what had happened in the harbor. I'll tell you, I couldn't believe I was alive.

There was a kind of air-raid shelter at this landing. The pilots
from Ford Island lived there. Now the wives of the men and officers who lived on Ford Island were around that morning. They
found some clean clothing and outfitted me. They wiped me
down a little bit and put me in some sports clothes. In five minutes the oil soaked through those clothes. I was just like a
soaped greasy rag. Then one of the wives said, "I know. There
are more clothes back here. The oil won't come through them."
So they put me in a navy captain's uniform with wings. Now
mind you, I was barefooted, with no hat, in formal dress, tails

and all. So I was Captain for a Day. I got a lot of respect around there. I was in my captain's uniform.

From there we went to the block arena and I slept in the arena that night. Then I went up to the marine barracks and they gave me a toothbrush and a razor. Three days later I was assigned to a destroyer, so I had another happy home. But every time somebody hollered boo or beat on the bulkhead I was about ready to jump over the side.

I might add that while I was waiting for the ship I had been assigned to there were a few small boats around. They were being taken here and there on chores of various kinds, so I, being a coxswain, was occasionally on one of these boats. A few men would go along with me. Three or four of us were making a trip and we stopped by the *Arizona*. They had put the fire out and things had cooled down enough for us to go aboard. It was pitiful. The decks were warped and there were bomb holes around. I went back into the turret I had been in. I retrieved the pair of shorts I had been wearing and the undershirt that I had crammed around the guns to keep the smoke out of the turret. I also found my cigarette lighter and knife and cigarette case, a few little things like that. But I didn't even look for the shoes; I never thought of it.

I can't believe there were any survivors below decks, because from midships forward the magazines had exploded internally. I later heard that the reason the magazines did not explode in the after part of the ship—the part I had been in—was because a fire-control man who was standing watch in the magazines had flooded them with water. If he hadn't done that there would have been very, very few survivors. I certainly wouldn't have survived if those magazines had gone up, and I don't think the others around me would have.

Nuclear Dawn

from World War II: War in the Pacific

Don Nardo

AFTER the United States captured the Japanese stronghold
of Okinawa in late June 1945, the Americans began prepara-
tions for the greatest undertaking of the war. Two sweeping military plans—Operation Olympic and Operation Coronet—would
begin the massive invasion of the Japanese home islands.
Kyushu, the southernmost large island in the group, would be
the first major target. American planners expected that the as-
sault would be time-consuming and bloody.

But the climactic invasion of Japan never occurred. Instead,
the war came to an abrupt and decisive end in a way no one
could have predicted. As soldiers died by the thousands on the
beaches of Iwo Jima and Okinawa, American scientists secretly
labored to put the finishing touches on the most terrifying
weapon ever devised. Only a handful of Americans and Allied
leaders knew that the scientists had been working on the device
since 1939.

Birth of the Manhattan Project

THE effort to develop an atomic bomb was code-named the
Manhattan Project. It was the culmination of a series of important scientific discoveries made in the 1920s and 1930s. Re-
searchers such as Albert Einstein, Danish physicist Niels Bohr,
and British physicist Ernest Rutherford studied the structure
and behavior of atoms, the tiny building blocks that make up all
matter. Among other things, they recognized that splitting
atoms of uranium and other radioactive elements released un-
usually large amounts of energy.

To escape Europe's Axis dictatorships, many of the world's
leading atomic scientists, including Einstein, Bohr, and Italy's
Enrico Fermi, moved to the United States in the late 1930s.
There, they continued with their research into the splitting of
the atom, called fission.

It did not take these scientists long to realize that the energy released during fission might be utilized in a weapon of enormous destructive power. The race to develop such a weapon began with a historic letter from Einstein to President Roosevelt on August 2, 1939. Einstein asserted:

> It may become possible to set up a nuclear chain reaction in a large mass of uranium, by which vast amounts of power . . . would be generated. . . . This new phenomenon would also lead to the construction of bombs. . . . A single bomb of this type, carried by boat and exploded in a port, might very well destroy the whole port, together with some of the surrounding territory.

Accepting Einstein's suggestion, Roosevelt and Winston Churchill immediately launched the huge and highly secret Manhattan Project. They felt there was good reason for haste. Allied spies reported that German scientists were also developing atomic bombs, which Hitler might use against Great Britain and eventually against the United States. This fear kept scientists working on the Manhattan Project at an ever-increasing pace. Many U.S. leaders also believed that the bomb was just what the country needed to quickly and decisively win the war.

The Roar That Warned of Doomsday

THE Manhattan Project was the most complex and costly scientific endeavor in history. It ended up costing the United States and Great Britain $2.5 billion, a tremendous sum at the time. The project involved scientists, military personnel, and labs all over the United States. Henry L. Stimson, secretary of war, headed the president's committee that decided how the bomb would be developed and delivered. Dr. J. Robert Oppenheimer led the scientific team, and Maj. Gen. Leslie R. Groves commanded the Army Corps of Engineers, whose task was to build the device. The government built two huge plants for bomb construction. One was in Oak Ridge, Tennessee, the other in Richland, Washington. Oppenheimer and his team of scientists worked at a special lab at Los Alamos in the desert near Santa Fe, New Mexico.

Security was tight. Although more than 200,000 people helped produce the bomb, only a tiny handful knew what they were actually working on. Even Vice President Truman knew nothing of the project until he was sworn in to succeed Roosevelt in April 1945. Those in charge made sure that it was the "best-kept secret of the war."

The atomic age began on July 16, 1945, when Oppenheimer's and Groves's units conducted a test firing of the new superweapon in the desert near Alamogordo, New Mexico. Although most of those working on the project believed the device would work, no one was prepared for the awesome power the weapon actually possessed. The large steel tower that held the bomb was completely vaporized in the first second of the explosion. Windows rattled 250 miles away, and a blinding light momentarily banished the early morning darkness. Gen. Thomas F. Farrell, who witnessed the test from a bunker five miles away, later described the spectacle:

> The effects could well be called . . . magnificent, beautiful, stupendous, and terrifying. . . . The lighting effects beggared description. The whole country was lighted . . . with an intensity many times that of the midday sun. It was golden, purple, violet, gray, and blue. . . . Thirty seconds after the explosion, came, first the air blast, pressing hard against people and things, . . . followed almost immediately by the strong, sustained, awesome roar which warned of doomsday and made us feel that we puny things were blasphemous to dare tamper with the forces heretofore [formerly] reserved to the Almighty.

Minutes after the test, President Truman received news of its success. The United States, he realized, now had nearly unlimited power at its disposal. But should the Americans unleash such destructive power on other human beings?

The Decision to Drop the Bomb

TRUMAN and his advisers considered several factors in deciding whether or not to use the new atomic device. A few of the president's advisers argued that using the bomb would be morally wrong. They pointed out that the weapon's blast would be so huge that there would be no way to avoid killing thousands of civilians while striking at military targets. They were also against using the bomb because it was not needed, they claimed. The ongoing blockade and bombing of Japanese cities had already nearly destroyed Japan. According to this view, it was only a matter of time before the enemy would have to surrender.

But Secretary Stimson and Truman were unmoved by these arguments. They had weighed the consequences of *not* using the bomb. U.S. strategists told the president that the invasion of Japan would take one year or more and would cost at least half a million American and several million Japanese lives. And Stimson pointed out that the Japanese would likely fight to the death. It was better, he said, to kill a few thousand with the bomb and end the war quickly than allow millions to die in an invasion. Also, he insisted, the United States should not be moved by moral considerations. After all, the Japanese had not been concerned about the morality of their sneak attack on Pearl Harbor, the savage mistreatment of American prisoners, and the brutal kamikaze attacks. Truman agreed and later wrote, "I regarded the bomb as a weapon and never had any doubt that it should be used." Winston Churchill sent word that he favored the bomb's use if it could bring an early end to the war.

Having determined that they would drop the bomb, the American leaders now had to choose the targets. Some said Kyoto, the ancient capital, should be destroyed first. But Stimson disagreed, pointing out that the city housed Japan's greatest cultural and religious shrines and, therefore, should be spared. Truman agreed, writing in his private journal, "Even if the Japs are savages, ruthless, merciless and fanatic, we as the leader of the free world for the common welfare cannot drop this terrible bomb on the old capital or the new [Tokyo]." The targets finally agreed upon were Hiroshima, Kikura, Niigata, and Nagasaki, all centers of industry and war production.

Flight of the *Enola Gay*

THE final series of events leading to the dropping of the atomic bomb went like clockwork. On July 24, 1945, the U.S. cruiser *Indianapolis* delivered lead buckets containing the uranium needed for the bomb to Tinian Island in the Marianas. The captain of the ship was unaware of the contents of the buckets. His orders were that if his ship sank, he should save the containers at all costs, putting them in lifeboats if necessary. That same day, planes from the United States arrived with other essential bomb parts. Scientists on Tinian assembled the first bomb, nicknamed Little Boy, during the next few days. They did not arm it, fearing that if the plane carrying it crashed during takeoff, the entire island would be blown up. They decided instead to arm the weapon in the air shortly before reaching the target.

On July 26, 1945, the United States and the Allies issued a final ultimatum to Japan, demanding unconditional surrender. The message concluded, "The alternative for Japan is prompt and utter destruction." When the Japanese refused, Truman grimly commented that there is "no alternative now."

On August 5, 1945, technicians on Tinian loaded the world's first nuclear weapon onto a B-29 called *Enola Gay*. The pilot, Col. Paul Tibbets, had named the plane after his mother. Two other B-29s, carrying military observers and cameras, would accompany the *Enola Gay*.

The planes glided off the Tinian runway at 2:45 A.M. on August 6. They reached the initial target, Hiroshima, a city of 340,000, at about 8:05 A.M. At exactly 8:15, the *Enola Gay*'s bombardier discharged the four-ton Little Boy, and the plane lurched upward in response to the sudden loss of weight. Tibbets then banked the plane away at a steep angle in order to avoid the effects of the coming blast. A few seconds later, the bomb automatically detonated, or exploded, at an altitude of eighteen hundred feet. An arc of blinding light seemed to tear the sky apart. "My God!" murmured a startled crew member. Another said, "Suddenly a glaring whitish pink light appeared in the sky accompanied by an unnatural tremor that was followed almost immediately by a wave of suffocating heat and wind that swept everything away in its path." As a gigantic mushroom cloud rose into the atmosphere, Tibbets swung the plane around for a better view. "It was like looking over a tar barrel boiling," he said. "We couldn't see the city at all through the thin layer of dust." In fact, there was little left to see. Most of Hiroshima had simply ceased to exist.

A Rain of Ruin

THE reactions to the bombing of Hiroshima were immediate and emotional. The shocked Japanese called the destruction "barbaric." Radio Tokyo reported: "The impact of the bomb is so terrific that practically all living things, human and animals, literally were seared to death by the tremendous heat and pressure engendered by the blast. All the dead and injured were burned beyond recognition." Early estimates suggested that more than seventy thousand people died in the initial blast alone. More perished each hour from serious injuries or in the fires that raged through the ruins. The Japanese leaders charged, "This diabolical weapon brands the United States for ages to come as a destroyer of justice and of mankind."

Truman announced the official U.S. position on August 7, saying, "The force from which the sun draws its power has been loosed upon those who brought war to the Far East." The president warned, "If they [the Japanese] do not now accept our terms, they may expect a rain of ruin from the air, the like of which has never been seen on this earth."

When the Japanese still did not surrender, a group of B-29s dropped a second atomic bomb two days later, on August 9. This time, the target was Nagasaki, a city of 250,000 located on the island of Kyushu. The nearly total destruction of the city sent a wave of fear through the country. Japanese leaders met that night to debate surrender. The most extreme militarists argued that the country should fight on. They insisted that every Japanese citizen should die rather than surrender. Those who felt that surrender was better than annihilation called upon Emperor Hirohito to decide. For years, the Japanese people had fought a bloody war for the honor of their "living god." Now, as they teetered on the brink of total destruction, their fate was in his hands.

Judith Steel
from Hiding to Survive
Maxine B. Rosenberg

Jews throughout Europe were persecuted during World War II. Millions were murdered as part of the Nazi party's plan to rid the world of the Jews. Here, Judith Steel tells of the courageous French family that saved her life by hiding her from the German secret police.

I'VE been told by relatives that in 1939, when I was fourteen months old, my parents, my grandfather, and I sailed for Cuba on the S.S. *St. Louis.* We were 4 of 936 Jews trying to escape from Germany before it was too late. Unbeknownst to us, the Cuban government had already notified the Germans that we could not enter their country. And the United States also refused to take us in.

When the ship returned to Europe, Jewish organizations paid England, France, Holland, and Belgium to accept a number of the people. My family went to a small town in southern France, where we rented an apartment in a little house. Others had no place to go and ended up back in Germany, where they were eventually sent to the camps.

At that time it was still safe for Jews in France, so we didn't hide our religion. At home we spoke German, but soon I learned French from Suzy, our landlord's daughter. She was four years older than I, and we played a lot together. I particularly loved going to her house because her mother was affectionate and gave me attention. I called her "Maman Suzy," which I thought meant "Suzy's mother" in French.

In 1942 the situation for Jews in France became so dangerous, my parents were afraid to leave the house. Maman Suzy would bring us chicken, milk, or potatoes from her friend's farm, but usually we went hungry.

My parents especially encouraged me then to visit Maman Suzy because she fed me. I'd stand outside her window and yell, "Maman Suzy, would you like me to come?"

She'd call out, "Yes, my little one. Come!"

One morning there was a loud knock on our door. It was the French police with orders to arrest my family. They put my parents and me on a truck and took us to Gurs, a camp where we were handed over to the Nazis. My grandfather, who was very sick in bed, was left behind.

For the next three weeks my mother and I lived in a crowded barrack while my father was somewhere else. One day my mother hugged me tightly and said, "You may never see Mommy and Daddy again." I could tell from her eyes that something was very wrong.

That night my father took me outside of the camp and brought me to a small room where there were a few other children. He pointed to a man who was holding out a drink and said, "Look at that." When I reached for the cup he let go of my hand. A second later he was gone. I started screaming.

The next morning Maman Suzy's husband, Josef, came for me. He said we were going to his house, where my grandfather was now living.

As soon as I saw Maman Suzy, I ran into her arms and cried. But she looked at me horrified. I had sores all over my body. Maman Suzy laid me across her lap and covered me with iodine. When that didn't help, she called the doctor. He knew I was Jewish but still came to the house to treat me. As he was leaving, I overheard him tell Maman Suzy I was in such bad condition from not eating that within a few weeks I would have died.

When I recovered, Maman Suzy said, "From now on, I'm going to be your mother." She was pregnant at the time and told me I'd be brought up just like one of her own children. Then she changed my last name to hers, Enard. After that, I was part of the family. Instead of calling her "Maman Suzy," I now called her "Maman," and Josef "Papa."

Both Maman and Papa treated me well, but I always felt closer to her. When she sang French songs, I was sure they were meant for me. A few months later Jacques was born. I considered him my brother and Suzy my sister.

Meanwhile my grandfather had a stroke and went to the hospital. I visited him there just once, and after that I never saw him again.

Now the only family I knew was Maman's, and I felt a part of it. I liked playing with the animals around the house and stood and watched Papa when he slaughtered pigs. I even ate the snails Maman cooked. And on Sundays I went to church with the family, singing the hymns and making the sign of the Cross.

That September I started kindergarten. Suzy and I told everybody at school we were sisters, and they believed us.

Meanwhile Maman told Suzy and me she was hiding an old Jewish artist named Lazarre in the attic. Whenever I'd go up there to get toys, I'd see him, but we rarely talked.

Soon it was summer, and Maman wanted to send me to the day camp that Suzy had been going to. It was run by nuns, but not those from the church we attended. On the day it started, Suzy and I walked there together. The priest didn't recognize me and asked Suzy who I was. She said I was the Jewish girl her parents were taking care of. When he heard that, the priest said he couldn't accept me because I would put the other children in danger. So that summer both Suzy and I stayed home.

Even though many of the people in town remembered I was Jewish from the time I had lived with my parents, Maman kept warning me to be careful. She said these people probably wouldn't turn me in, but if the wrong person found out, we all could be killed. She told me I had to keep quiet about my past. The only time I felt open and free was with the family. They made me feel safe and wanted.

Still, I was hoping my parents would come back for me, and often asked Maman when that day would be. She'd say, "In time, my child. Right now this is your home." And I accepted it. I felt so comfortable, I soon forgot a war was going on.

But one day in 1944, while Suzy and I were out wheeling Jacques in his carriage, we heard gunshots coming from the center of town. Suddenly people started running in all directions. Suzy and I grabbed Jacques and raced into a jewelry store, where we stayed until it got quiet.

The next day German soldiers arrived at our house and took over Papa's furniture factory, which was connected to where we lived. They said that now Papa had to work for them.

Since I had a slight German accent, Maman was terrified. She worried that the soldiers might wonder why a German child was living with a French family. "If they realize you are Jewish, we'll all be dead," she said. She warned me not to speak when the soldiers were nearby.

I listened to what Maman said, and when the soldiers were around, I stood there and smiled without saying a word. At first it was like a game, but when I noticed their guns, I shook inside.

Sometimes I understood what the soldiers were saying. One said in German that I was pretty and looked just like Maman. Later I said to Maman, "See, I *am* your child."

Meanwhile I was still going to school and playing outdoors to make everything appear normal. But the longer the soldiers were in the town, the more nervous Maman and Papa became. Maman suddenly decided I looked Jewish because my ears stuck out too much. She decided to cover them by pulling my hair tightly over the tops, and she combed Suzy's hair the same way. She practically dressed Suzy and me alike, too. Having the same coloring as Maman, we sort of resembled each other, which Maman hoped made me less noticeable to the Germans.

One night from my bedroom I overheard Maman and Papa talking about the camps and saying they thought my father had died. Since they didn't mention my mother, I asked Maman the next morning when she would be coming back. Maman didn't give me a definite answer, so I expected my mother to arrive on my birthday, which was in February.

At the end of August 1944 the Germans who had been around our house for a few months suddenly told us they were leaving and said good-bye. Right after that France was liberated. Two days later Maman said that Lazarre had gone too, as had the four other Jews who had been hiding in the attic. I hadn't even known they were there.

Now that the war was over, I started thinking more about my mother and kept waiting for her to come. But it didn't happen. So for the next year and a half, I stayed with Maman, believing, This is where I'll live forever. Then one day she told me I was going to the United States to live with my aunt and uncle. She said that they were rich people and would give me a good life.

I was crushed. Here I had no parents, and now I was being taken away from Maman. I loved her, and I knew she loved me. She was always kind and protected me. I begged to stay with her, but she said it was impossible.

Maman took me to a Jewish organization in Paris that was temporarily caring for sixty-eight children whose papers were being made ready for passage to America. The few weeks I was there, Maman visited. Right before I left for America she came to say good-bye. When she hugged and kissed me, I couldn't stop screaming, I was so frightened.

After ten days on the seas the ship docked, and I was met by my aunt and uncle and their two sons. I felt totally lost. I didn't know who they were, and I couldn't speak English, their language.

It was hard for me, and for them too. The first year I only wanted to be with Maman. I missed her so much. But as time went on, I got used to my new family and felt at home with them.

For years and years I didn't contact Maman, and she didn't get in touch with me. But she was still on my mind. She had been special. I never forgot her.

from

Red-Tail Angels

Patricia and Fredrick McKissack

After decades of discrimination, the first African Americans were admitted to the Army Air Corps in 1941. Known as the Red-Tail Angels, these men fought valiantly for freedom at a time when their own freedom was often denied. Their success laid the groundwork for the end of segregation in the United States military.

GIVEN the history of poor treatment in the military, blacks had good reason to avoid military service, but there were always sufficient numbers of blacks who were willing to serve in the army and navy. When the United States entered World War I, African-American leaders, such as W. E. B. Du Bois, encouraged young black men to forget about the internal struggle and "close ranks" with white Americans for the common good of the country. And, once again, 375,000 men—from Mississippi sharecroppers to Chicago English professors—enlisted and served in four all-black units.

Nicknamed the Hell Fighters by the Germans, the men of the celebrated 369th fought in the trenches for 191 days, under heavy fire, yet they never retreated or had a member captured.

At the same time African-Americans were risking their lives to defend democracy, the United States Army issued a memorandum to the French command, asking them to prevent any "pronounced degree of intimacy" between French and African-American soldiers. The memo further requested that the French should not "eat with Negroes, shake hands or seek to meet with them outside of military service." But most of all, the French were asked not "to commend black soldiers too highly in the presence of white Americans."

The French responded by giving the entire 369th Regiment the croix de guerre, a high French military award. And Privates Needham Roberts and Henry Johnson, members of the 369th, were individually decorated with the croix de guerre for their heroism. Soldiers from other black regiments were also awarded honors.

The armistice was signed on November 11, 1918. The "war to

end all wars" was over. As was the case in previous wars, proud black soldiers returned home hopeful that their honorable service and outstanding displays of courage and discipline would translate into respect for them at home. But they were wrong.

Despite their performance and character, black soldiers were not accepted or respected by the military or by the civilian communities to which they returned. Preaching hatred and fear, groups such as the reorganized Ku Klux Klan conjured up visions of a well-trained "black army," against which the white race needed to defend itself.

During the summer of 1919 seventy-six blacks were lynched, some of them servicemen still in their uniforms. Whites rioted in twenty-five cities and savagely beat and killed innocent women and children. They burned African-American businesses and schools. Out of the ashes of the "Red Summer" of 1919 emerged a new African-American whose militancy was captured by Claude McKay, a young poet, who wrote "If We Must Die":

> If we must die, let it not be like hogs
> Hunted and penned in an inglorious spot,
> While round us bark the mad and hungry dogs,
> Making their mock at our accursed lot.
> If we must die, O let us nobly die,
> So that our precious blood may not be shed
> In vain; then even the monsters we defy
> Shall be constrained to honor us though dead!
> O kinsmen! we must meet the common foe!
> Though far outnumbered let us show us brave,
> And for their thousand blows deal one deathblow!
> What though before us lies the open grave?
> Like men we'll face the murderous, cowardly pack,
> Pressed to the wall, dying, but fighting back!

Between the two wars, the Great Depression plunged the nation into an economic abyss. Whites were poor, and blacks were poorer still. The whole economic picture was bleak. Some whites chose military careers because it offered them a way out of their grinding poverty. Black men tried the same avenue of escape, but the peacetime army and navy turned them away.

The army and navy made it clear that they didn't want black volunteers except in menial positions. During the early 1930s, the number of black soldiers in the regular army dwindled to the lowest level since the Civil War. Then when the Army and

Navy Air Corps became integral parts of the U.S. military, men of all races and nationalities were drawn to the drama and excitement of airplanes. But African-American men were not admitted to the air divisions because of the prevailing racial attitudes of the civilian population.

The military establishment chose to believe African-Americans were not smart enough or disciplined enough to fly combat aircraft, even though black pilots had distinguished themselves in the French Air Force during World War I. To support their false assumptions, military officials concocted an infamous report issued by the War College in 1925.

The report stated that African-Americans were "a subspecies of the human population" and probably "the worst of all races." It was impossible, in the opinion of the report, for them to be good officers. The army interpreted the report to mean that blacks could not be pilots. The infamous report managed to ignore the accomplishments of black military heroes and such outstanding pilots as Bessie Coleman, William Powell, Willa Brown, Cornelius Coffey, John C. Robinson, and the World War I flying ace Eugene Bullard (about whom a film was made in 1926 titled *The Flying Ace*). All the assertions in the report were made without one shred of scientific proof, yet it was accepted as truth, until March 1942, when five African-American men earned their silver wings at Tuskegee Army Air Field in Alabama.

These five black pilots were part of an "experiment," designed as a result of pressure put on the War Department by African-American leaders and the press. Their persistent demands for the admission of blacks in the Army Air Corps paid off in early 1941. The secretary of war reluctantly approved a plan to establish the all-black 99th Fighter Squadron and to construct an air base located in Tuskegee, Alabama, where other black pilots could be trained.

The experimental program was designed to fail. But against all odds, young black men from all over the country, most with two years of college or more, proved to a doubtful nation that they could fly airplanes. Then to their dismay, the question became, "How will they fare in combat?" The answer is a matter of history.

By 1946, over 992 black pilots (not including ground crews) had been trained at the segregated facilities at Tuskegee Army Air Field (TAAF). From 1942 until the end of the war, many of these men served in the all-black 332nd Fighter Group, composed of the original 99th, 100th, 301st, and 302nd Fighter Squadrons.

Although the black fighters got off to a shaky start, as they gained confidence they flew hundreds of successful missions over North Africa and Europe, eventually gaining the respect and admiration of the military brass who had questioned their ability and doubted their courage. Known fondly as the Red-Tail Angels because of the red markings on the tails of their aircraft, these pioneer pilots earned a reputation for never losing a bomber they escorted. In addition, they brought home 150 Distinguished Flying Crosses and Legions of Merit. Sixty-six pilots died in aerial combat, defending the rights of others—rights they themselves did not enjoy. But their sacrifices were not in vain.

The accomplishments of the Tuskegee pilots, navigators, and crewmen helped defeat Nazi tyranny and set an inspiring example of courage and competence to people around the world, and in so doing hastened the end of segregation in the military and in civilian society.

A Daughter of the Sea

Maureen Crane Wartski

"HEY, Mr. Manning, can't we go fishing? It'd be a lot more fun than collecting creepy crawlies."

Lien didn't pretend to laugh with the rest of the group as Curt Hanson clowned around. She didn't feel like laughing. In fact, she wished she'd never come on this Saturday outing with her high school Biology Club.

During the long ride from Brockton to Orleans on the Cape, she'd been totally ignored. Except for the club adviser, Mr. Manning, no one had even spoken to her. It was as if Lien Huan didn't exist.

A strong sea-wind whipped Lien's long black hair as she climbed out of the van and walked some distance from the others to look at the sea. A September storm had lashed Cape Cod the previous night, and the sea beyond the dunes was still fretful. As she watched white-frothed waves pummel the shore, Lien could almost hear Grandpa relating his favorite sea story.

"On the morning that terrible voyage began," she imagined him saying, "the sea was like a raging demon. 'Come, sons and daughters of the sea,' it roared at us, 'do you dare to start the longest journey of your lives?'"

"Lien?" Mr. Manning's voice broke into her thoughts. "Lien, you're far away. Are you woolgathering?"

Low, so that Mr. Manning couldn't hear, Curt Hanson snickered, "That's what happens to slopes when they eat too much dog meat."

Lien's hands closed into fists before she remembered that Curt outweighed her by about a hundred pounds. Besides, fighting just made for more trouble. It was because her older brother had started getting into fights and running with a gang that the Huan family had moved to Brockton.

But there were troubles here in Brockton, too, and big-mouthed Curt Hanson was only one of them. There was the GOOKS, GET OUT sign that had been spray-painted on the steps of the house that Ma and Papa rented along with Uncle Dac and Aunty Hong. Rotten eggs had been smeared all over the driveway a week after they moved in, and the windows of the convenience store that the family had bought had been smashed many times over. And then there were the Huans' neighbors—most of them indifferent, a few friendly, many definitely hostile.

School was no different. The teachers tried—Mr. Manning, especially, went out of his way to be helpful—but Lien had found that only the Asian kids were friendly. It was Ahn Doh, one of the Vietnamese girls she'd met, who had convinced her to join the Biology Club. Because she was interested in biology and liked Mr. Manning, Lien had agreed.

But Ahn hadn't come on today's field trip, and without her, Lien felt very much alone. She skimmed her eyes over the other students who made up the Biology Club. She didn't know Mitch Kennedy or Naomi Barnett, but fair-haired, freckled Shani Moore was in Lien's freshman biology class, and Debby Olivera sat across from her in English. Besides a perfunctory "hi," neither of the girls had bothered to talk to Lien.

And then there was Curt Hanson. Lien sighed. Unfortunately for her, Curt was in her homeroom, and each morning he went out of his way to antagonize her. Even more unfortunately Curt, who wasn't even a member of the Biology Club, today had tagged along with his friend Mitch.

Perhaps Mr. Manning had heard Curt's obnoxious comments? But apparently he hadn't because he was saying, "All right, today we're going to catalog organisms that live in the tide pools. Low tide is an hour from now, so until then we can do our bit for ecology and pick up six-pack holders and anything that could hurt wildlife. We'll break into two groups."

Please, please let me be in Mr. Manning's group—but he was saying, "Naomi and Debby, you're with me. Shani, Lien, and Mitch, you're a team. You, too, Curt."

"Why can't we pick our own teams?" Curt protested.

Mr. Manning ignored this. "We'll go left, you go right. We'll meet back at the van in an hour. Have fun."

"Yeah, right," Curt muttered as the teacher walked away. "Some fun when we're stuck with Miss Saigon."

She didn't have to stand here listening to his insults. Turning on her heel, Lien started down the dunes. She was halfway down when Curt came barreling down and nearly knocked her over. "Why don't you watch where you're going?" she cried.

Like a rattlesnake poised to strike, he wheeled to face her. "No," he snarled, "*you* watch out."

"This is a free country," Lien wanted to retort, but the look in Curt's pale blue eyes silenced her.

"You gooks come here to *our* country and take all the jobs.

You stink up everything. You people make me sick, so just get out of my face."

Something inside Lien hardened into ice. She couldn't move or speak as Mitch said uncertainly, "Hey, Curt, lighten up."

No one else said anything. Not looking at any of them, Lien walked stiff-legged down the sand dunes onto the beach. Her heart was pounding like a jackhammer, her legs were rubbery, and angry tears made her eyes feel as though they were full of grit.

Since leaving Boston, Lien had become used to unshed tears. You didn't waste time crying in the Huan family because there was no time *to* waste. For Lien, there was school, and there was the store. Everyone in the family worked in the store. Even Grandpa would putter around and smoke his pipe and wait on the Vietnamese customers. Whenever anyone would listen to him, he'd tell stories about his fishing days and relate how he had sailed his boat across the South China Sea.

Once, only once, Lien had complained to her mother about school. "*Thoi-dii*—stop, and think what you are saying," Ma had said in her practical way. "Life in America is good. You don't know what real hardship is, fortunately."

Maybe not, Lien thought now as she walked along the deserted beach, but over and over she'd heard the story of how her family had left Vietnam on Grandpa's rickety old fishing boat. The Huans had almost starved on that horrendous journey, but somehow they had kept alive, and by some miracle Grandpa had managed to evade pirates and survive storms till they made landfall in Hong Kong.

Lien had been born in a Hong Kong refugee camp. She had been just a baby when the family came to America. Papa had owned a small store in Vietnam before the Communists came, but the family had been nearly penniless when they finally reached America.

For a while they'd depended on the charity of the church that had sponsored them and set them up in a small Boston apartment—but not for long. The Huans had worked hard: Papa and Uncle Dac in a factory, Ma and Aunty Hong at cleaning people's houses, Grandpa in a restaurant washing dishes.

"*Cho, cho.*" Grandpa always chuckled when he told Lien this story. "Wait and be patient, I told them all. We are tired and sad now, but that will change. For sons and daughters of the sea, there are always new horizons."

But sometimes patience didn't help. Lien wiped her eyes with the back of her hand and looked back over her shoulder. Noting that her so-called team had stopped to examine something on the beach, she looked toward the sea again.

That was when she saw the fish. It lay sleek and dark like a large exclamation point in the breakers not far from shore. As Lien watched, it began to swim about. A shark in a feeding frenzy? she wondered, nervously.

Now the fish was swimming closer to shore, and something about the way it moved made Lien catch her lower lip in her teeth. She wished she knew more about fish, wished that Grandpa were there. He would surely know what was happening.

She turned and shouted to the others in her group. Curt and Mitch didn't look up, but Shani Moore did. When she saw Lien waving, she said something to the others and came running over.

"There's a big fish in the water!" Lien called out to her.

"What fish?" Shani began, then caught her breath. "Oh," she gasped. "Wow. What is it? Do you know?"

Lien shook her head. "A shark?"

The boys had now come up, and Curt scoffed, "That's no shark—it's a whale. My father knows all about fish. He told me whales are so stupid, they swim up onshore and die."

"It's a pilot whale," Mitch corrected. "I saw a show about them on TV last year. They sometimes get confused and beach themselves."

"It *looks* confused—like it's swimming in circles," Shani said. "Can't we do something to help it?"

"*Nada*—zip." Curt, Lien realized, was enjoying being the voice of authority. "Once that sucker beaches, it'll die."

"I'll get Mr. Manning." Mitch took off down the beach and returned a short while later with the rest of the group and the club adviser, who mused, "One pilot whale all alone—looks like a very young calf, from the size of it. It must have become disoriented and wandered away from its pod during last night's storm. Now it doesn't know how to get back to the open sea."

"Can't we get it turned around?" Lien asked. Curt snorted in disgust, but Mr. Manning nodded.

"We can try," he said. "Listen up, now. Lien, you and Shani go to the nearest house and call the police. Tell them that you've found a pilot whale in the shallows and ask them to contact the New England Aquarium and also the Center for Coastal Studies in Provincetown. Have you got that? The rest of us will try to keep the whale from beaching."

As Lien climbed the dunes, she couldn't keep the image of the lost young whale out of her mind. Once again she wished that Grandpa were with them.

"What can your grandfather do?" Shani wondered, and Lien realized she'd spoken her last thought aloud.

"He used to be a fisherman," she explained. "He's always talking about fish."

"My grandmother's a talker, too," Shani volunteered. "She lives with us. It drives my mom crazy, but I like it when she tells stories about when she was a girl in Ireland."

"My grandpa lives with us, too. Sometimes he calls me 'daughter of the sea'—" Lien stopped short. Shani didn't care about Grandpa or his stories. Perhaps she'd laugh—but instead, Shani looked surprised.

"I guess grandparents are all alike, huh? I never knew Cambodians before—"

"Vietnamese," Lien corrected. She couldn't help adding, "What do you mean, you don't know us? We're all over school."

"I mean, I don't *know* you," Shani explained. "I've seen you around school, sure, but you always stick with your own friends—"

She broke off as a patrol car drove slowly down the road. Shani flagged it down and explained what had happened. "I'll get on it right away," the policeman promised. Then he added, "I remember one winter storm when thirty whales got beached."

"What happened to them?" Lien asked uneasily.

"I think volunteers managed to save some," the policeman said, vaguely.

Perhaps Curt was right after all, Lien thought as she and Shani hurried back toward the beach. Perhaps—

"Lien, look!" Shani exclaimed.

Lien's heart sank. They had reached the sea again, and in the short time that they had been away, the tide had ebbed considerably. The lost whale was now struggling in much shallower water. Mr. Manning, together with Mitch, Debby, and Naomi, was standing waist deep in the surf and apparently attempting to turn the creature around.

Curt sat on a pile of rocks, massaging his ankle. "I sprained it," he complained when Shani asked him what was the matter. Then he added sullenly, "I'm not even a member of your stupid club, and anyway, it's a waste of time. Once a whale starts to strand, it's history."

Ignoring Curt, Shani waded into the water. Lien followed. Though the September sun was warm, the sea was so cold on her bare legs that she cried out with shock. Then she gasped again as the whale smacked the water with its tail and doused her with spume.

"Turn him around—turn him!" Mr. Manning was shouting. "Lien, Shani, grab hold of him! Try to push him toward the open sea!"

Determinedly, Lien waded up to her waist, then stopped. She didn't want to touch, let alone take hold of, the big, slimy creature. As she hesitated, it turned in the water and rubbed against her.

The sleek, dark skin wasn't slippery! It felt like wet suede cloth. And it was making soft, squealing noises—scared noises. Without further thought, Lien grabbed as much of the whale as she could and tried to help the others point it toward the open sea.

"Turn, willya?" Mitch was pleading. "Don't you want to join your friends?"

For a second it seemed as if the whale had gotten the message, and they all cheered as it began to swim toward the open sea. But a few minutes later it turned around and once more headed for the shore.

"Why does he keep *doing* that?" Lien asked as they splashed toward it.

Wiping away the salt spray from his eyes, Mr. Manning explained that no one really knew why pilot whales beach themselves. "Their guidance system might get disoriented by a storm or by some kind of geomagnetic field sent out by submerged rocks," he said. "Anyway, this little guy has double trouble. Pilot whales are social creatures who live in a pod—a community of whales. They depend on each other for help and company. Junior probably couldn't even survive without his friends."

"Then even if we get 'Junior' back into the sea, he'll die," Shani said unhappily.

"He'll certainly die if he's beached. Whales are mammals, but they're made to float in the water. On dry land, Junior's internal organs would very likely be crushed by his own weight." Mr. Manning added, "But don't give up hope, crew. The New England Aquarium has saved whales like our Junior before this. We just have to keep him from beaching himself until they get here."

He broke off as the whale's tail whapped down on the water, practically drowning its would-be rescuers. "One more time, group!" Mr. Manning ordered. "Let's try to get him turned around!"

Lien dug her toes into the sand and grabbed hold of the

young whale's flipper. "You *have* to try!" she shouted at him. "You're a son of the sea, darn it."

Junior tried to dive in the shallow water. The others let go, but Lien stayed with him. "Brave whale, big whale, go back to the sea," she commanded.

Her words ended in a shriek as Junior shook loose and knocked her off her feet into the water. Lien came up, sputtering, and saw the young whale heading for shore once again.

Lien lost track of time. Over and over, they caught and pointed Junior in the right direction, only to have him swim back toward the shore. They tried the exercise until Lien's arms ached, and she was exhausted by the time a police cruiser arrived. With it was a truckful of men and women in wet suits.

"Reinforcements," Mr. Manning groaned, thankfully. "About time, too."

Mr. Manning stayed back to talk with the volunteers, but the others waded to shore and huddled into blankets that the police had brought along. Lien took a paper cup of hot coffee in almost numb hands and went to sit on a rock nearest the sea. After a few moments, Shani joined her.

"I don't think I'll ever be warm again," Shani complained through chattering teeth, "and I ache everywhere."

"My arms and legs feel like they're going to fall off," Lien agreed. "How long were we in there with Junior, anyway?"

Shani shook her head. Then she asked, "What was all that weird stuff you were talking about back there?"

Lien felt embarrassed. "Grandpa says things like that all the time," she mumbled. "I guess I was thinking aloud, trying to psych Junior out."

"Poor guy. He just wants to go home." Shani sighed. "He just doesn't know how."

As she spoke, a van bearing a familiar logo drove onto the beach. Scientists from the New England Aquarium had arrived! When a veterinarian waded into the surf to check Junior's condition, Lien threw off her blanket and followed him.

She held her breath with the rest until the vet declared, "I think we can save this one. We'll take him back to the Aquarium's Animal Care Center."

"All *ri-ight!*" Shani exulted, while the others whooped aloud.

The veterinarian was beaming, too. "We got lucky this time. This whale is very young. If all goes well, we'll keep him till he matures and eventually release him."

Lien remembered Junior's mournful, frightened cries. "But

will he be able to survive away from his pod?" she asked anxiously.

"We'll release him near another whale community that will take him in," the veterinarian explained. He then added, "It's a good thing you found him when you did and kept him from actually beaching and hurting himself."

"Lien was the one who spotted him," Mr. Manning said, and Lien felt a warm glow until she heard Curt's snort. That derisive sound reminded her that nothing had really changed.

As Junior's rescue swung into gear, Mr. Manning marched the soaked Biology Club to dry land. "It's going to take a while before they get Junior away," he said. "If we want to hang around, we have to get out of these wet clothes. The scuba divers brought along some extra sweats we can borrow. We can change in the rest rooms near the beach parking lot."

As they followed their adviser up the dunes, Lien turned back to look at the sea. She saw that Junior was being fitted into a harness that would lift him onto a bed in a waiting back-loader. He was lucky, she thought. It was apparently easy for a displaced whale to find acceptance with a new group of friends, whereas humans—

"Saying good-bye to your fishy friend, slope-head?" Curt sneered in one of his carrying whispers.

Lien froze—but then Shani snapped, "Shut up, Curt. You are *such* a jerk."

"Yeah, Curt," Mitch agreed, and one of the girls—Debby Olivera—added, "It's not funny. We all care about Junior."

Once more Lien's eye felt gritty, but these were happy tears. Through them, she smiled at her new friends.

Someday, she was sure, a strong Junior would return to the open sea and join his new pod. And as for her—wasn't she also a daughter of the sea?

The Stonecutter

A Japanese Folk Tale

ONCE upon a time there lived a stonecutter, who went every day to a great rock in the side of a big mountain and cut out slabs for gravestones or for houses. He understood very well the kinds of stones wanted for the different purposes, and as he was a careful workman he had plenty of customers. For a long time he was quite happy and contented, and asked for nothing better than what he had.

Now in the mountain dwelt a spirit which now and then appeared to men, and helped them in many ways to become rich and prosperous. The stonecutter, however, had never seen this spirit, and only shook his head, with an unbelieving air, when anyone spoke of it. But a time was coming when he learned to change his opinion.

One day the stonecutter carried a gravestone to the house of a rich man, and saw there all sorts of beautiful things, of which he had never even dreamed. Suddenly his daily work seemed to grow harder and heavier, and he said to himself: "Oh, if only I were a rich man, and could sleep in a bed with silken curtains and golden tassels, how happy I should be!"

And a voice answered him: "Your wish is heard; a rich man you shall be!"

At the sound of the voice the stonecutter looked round, but could see nobody. He thought it was all his fancy, and picked up his tools and went home, for he did not feel inclined to do any more work that day. But when he reached the little house where he lived, he stood still with amazement, for instead of his wooden hut was a stately palace filled with splendid furniture, and most splendid of all was the bed, in every respect like the one he had envied. He was nearly beside himself with joy, and in his new life the old one was soon forgotten.

It was now the beginning of summer, and each day the sun blazed more fiercely. One morning the heat was so great that the stonecutter could scarcely breathe, and he determined he would stop at home till the evening. He was rather dull, for he had never learned how to amuse himself, and was peeping through the closed blinds to see what was going on in the street, when a little carriage passed by, drawn by servants dressed in blue and silver. In the carriage sat a prince, and over his head a golden umbrella was held, to protect him from the sun's rays.

"Oh, if I were only a prince!" said the stonecutter to himself, as the carriage vanished round the corner. "Oh, if I were only a prince, and could go in such a carriage and have a golden umbrella held over me, how happy I should be!"

And the voice of the mountain spirit answered: "Your wish is heard; a prince you shall be."

And a prince he was. Before his carriage rode one company of men and another behind it; servants dressed in scarlet and gold bore him along, the coveted umbrella was held over his head, everything heart could desire was his. But yet it was not enough. He looked round still for something to wish for, and when he saw that in spite of the water he poured on his grass the rays of the sun scorched it, and that in spite of the umbrella held over his head each day his face grew browner and browner, he cried in his anger: "The sun is mightier than I; oh, if I were only the sun!"

And the mountain spirit answered: "Your wish is heard; the sun you shall be."

And the sun he was, and felt himself proud in his power. He shot his beams above and below, on earth and in heaven; he burned up the grass in the fields and scorched the faces of princes as well as of poorer folk. But in a short time he began to grow tired of his might, for there seemed nothing left for him to do. Discontent once more filled his soul, and when a cloud covered his face, and hid the earth from him, he cried in his anger: "Does the cloud hold captive my rays, and is it mightier than I? Oh, that I were a cloud, and mightier than any!"

And the mountain spirit answered: "Your wish is heard; a cloud you shall be!"

And a cloud he was, and lay between the sun and the earth. He caught the sun's beams and held them, and to his joy the earth grew green again and flowers blossomed. But that was not enough for him, and for days and weeks he poured forth rain till the rivers overflowed their banks, and the crops of rice stood in water. Towns and villages were destroyed by the power of the rain, only the great rock on the mountainside remained unmoved. The cloud was amazed at the sight, and cried in wonder: "Is the rock, then, mightier than I? Oh, if I were only the rock!"

And the mountain spirit answered: "Your wish is heard; the rock you shall be!"

And the rock he was, and gloried in his power. Proudly he

stood, and neither the heat of the sun nor the force of the rain could move him. "This is better than all" he said to himself. But one day he heard a strange noise at his feet, and when he looked down to see what it could be, he saw a stonecutter driving tools into his surface. Even while he looked a trembling feeling ran all through him, and a great block broke off and fell upon the ground. Then he cried in his wrath: "Is a mere child of earth mightier than a rock? Oh, if I were only a man!"

And the mountain spirit answered: "Your wish is heard. A man once more you shall be!"

And a man he was, and in the sweat of his brow he toiled again at his trade of stonecutting. His bed was hard and his food scanty, but he had learned to be satisfied with it, and did not long to be something or somebody else. And as he never asked for things he had not got, or desired to be greater and mightier than other people, he was happy at last, and heard the voice of the mountain spirit no longer.

Acknowledgments *(continued from p. ii)*

Lucent Books, Inc.

"Nuclear Dawn" from *World War II: War in the Pacific* by Don Nardo. Copyright 1991 by Lucent Books. Reprinted with permission of Lucent Books, Inc.

McElderry Books, an imprint of Simon & Schuster Children's Publishing Division

Journey Home by Yoshiko Uchida is reprinted with the permission of Margaret K. McElderry Books, an imprint of Simon & Schuster Children's Publishing Division. Text copyright © 1978 Yoshiko Uchida.

Naval Institute Press

"No More War Games" by James Leamon Forbis from *The Pacific War Remembered: An Oral History Collection*, edited by John T. Mason, Jr. Used by permission of Naval Institute Press.

Walker and Company

From *Red-Tail Angels*. Copyright © 1995 by Patricia and Frederick McKissack. Reprinted with permission from Walker and Company, 435 Hudson Street, New York, NY 10014.

Note: Every effort has been made to locate the copyright owner of material reprinted in this book. Omissions brought to our attention will be corrected in subsequent editions.